School Floors

Effective perceptual movement programs
for your classroom

Barbara Pheloung

School Floors

by Barbara Pheloung

ISBN 0 9581608 4 8

National Library of Australia Cataloging-in-Publication data

Layout and design by Velvet Creative (www.velvet.com.au)

Printed and bound in Australia by Hyde Park Press Pty Ltd

Black and white illustrations by Tony Strachan

Published by Iceform Pty Ltd as trustee for the Pheloung Family Trust

Acknowledgements

The main characteristic of all the people who contributed to the book is that they are all smart enough to realise how little they know. They are the people who amount to something and change other people's lives. People like me who are show-offs and extroverts often just have fun in life but don't usually write books – too hard to sit down and be alone so much. I wouldn't have written anything if it hadn't been for my husband, Barry, who 'managed me'. One minute he would say "Barb, if you don't stop working so hard you'll kill yourself." The next minute, "Have you called that Mr. Smith yet?" It was Barry who bought my first computer, put it on my desk and suggested sweetly that I needed to write a book – my first painful pregnancy of a vision. But thank you my darling for your faith in me who 'didn't know anything.'

First of all I dedicate this book to Sister Yvonne Mary Ellis of the Sacred Heart Convent in Kensington. I want everyone to know what an influence she has been in all of this, not only just on me. It has been such an honour for me to travel with her.

The journey we have had could not have been taken alone. It is too hard to travel a new road on your own because there aren't many people to ask for directions and most people think you are a bit daft to be on it at all. In the early days Sister and I didn't know that there were others taking a similar lonely path and even when they lived in Australia we had never heard anything about them. It was only when I was racing around most of Australia and New Zealand to publicise my first book in 1986, did I hear of these other compatible travellers. And the amazing thing I found was that nobody knew where anyone else was travelling even when they were in the same State. **Networking! We needed to network.**

The next person I would like to acknowledge is my dear gifted, dyslexic daughter, Jini. I couldn't have possibly had a better editor and even though she herself has had many struggles she was able to help me with my dyslexia. There you go! I've said it – for the first time publicly. I always failed spelling, not too bad in English, struggled in Latin and French and top of the class in Mathematics and Science. Jini's gifts and struggles were not the same as mine but for her to have been able to back me up in such a magnificent way is almost unbelievable. It's like a flowering in both of our lives.

Veronica Steer has given all of us such a beautiful gift of her understanding of the true nature of Learning Difficulties and how our growing knowledge of how the brain and body cannot be thought of as two separate entities. She has contributed so much in checking and double checking my bursts of fluency and kept things accurate. We have had many hours of struggling over the putting together of this book considering we are like everybody else with patches of Learning Difficulties ourselves.

Dr. Marilyn Dyson deserves special mention because of her ground breaking digging into the mysteries of gut problems and food and chemical intolerances. She was discipled by the late, extraordinary Dr. Mary Lou Sheil who would have been very proud of her. So few people know the intricacies and the huge importance of treatment in this area and Marilyn has so generously shared her knowledge. I hope that her high-content article will be reproduced and translated for everyone (including doctors) all around the world – what a gift she has given us!

Jill Taylor (King) also occupies the place of an honourable pioneer. I was so fortunate to have had her as a partner in the Beach House because she was truly open minded and able to approach our subject in much the same way then as we do now. Her wonderful training as a Feldenkrais Practitioner together with her Physiotherapy expertise made a unique contribution. I also want to thank her for suggesting that I should write another book – this one. I hadn't really thought of doing that until she mentioned it.

A special thanks as well to Svea Gold. We have never met except on the Internet but when I read her book, *If Kids Just Came with Instruction Sheets* and watched her video on Autism, I knew immediately that I would have loved travelling with her. I greatly admire the painstaking work she has done to research everything she says. I never had the patience to do that. Thank you Svea for writing my Preface.

Of inspired help is my wonderful illustrator, Tony Strachan. His career has been as a dancer, actor, writer, theatre director and artist, (of course). He has risen to the many challenges I have flung his way. "Tony, can you draw me a baby with two generals who are arguing inside his head?" Thank you, Tony, for climbing aboard at the last minute, so to speak, finding time to do this as well as being the General Manager of the Australian Theatre of the Deaf.

All the other contributors who have written a section or more for this book have been specially unique to me. Each has their own way of looking at this subject and adds a flavour to the book which could not have been achieved on my own. It means that there will be something for everyone in my book and as a team I don't think very much has been missed. They have been acknowledged where they have been included in the book. All of us want all of you to take anything you like from this book for any seminar, magazine, parent newsletter, Teacher's journal etc. All you need to include with what you use is the name of this book, my company *Move to Learn*, my name and the name of the author of what you reprint. And then write us an email to tell us what you have done. **We will eventually win the war against the ignorance of the true neurological nature of the whole spectrum of Learning Difficulties.**

In almost every book that I have ever read, the author apologises to their loved ones, their staff and wonderfully helpful friends who have read the book for them, for being irritable and hard to get along with during the whole writing process. To me it is like having a baby. I can remember the insemination. I nearly aborted this one. And then, of course, you get fragile and tired and irritable. All I can say is that I do feel great sympathy for you all and ask for your forgiveness, especially to Stacey, Caroline, Gerry and Rick. But it is born now and I'm cleaning it up, hugging it, looking at its toes with marvel and hoping that it is going to be a well integrated individual book.

Barbara Anne Pheloung (nicknamed Bubbles and Brandy)

Preface

There are the scientists who work on nerve-growth factors and map the functions of the brain. Their latest research even pinpointed the conditions that create reading problems. They interpret MRIs and PET scans and they have finally admitted that the brain is plastic and can be changed. They win Nobel Prizes.

Then there are the Ministers of Education, the Education Tsars appointed by the government who try to legislate school success. And they have proven that it can't be done. In the U.S. children - under pressure - read to the expected standard in Elementary School (the first three years of school), but in Middle School, 50% can't read the demanded material, and in High School, 80% can't follow the requirements of the curriculum.

And then there are pioneers like Barbara Pheloung and those who explore and study with her. They are the mothers and Teachers who quietly and stubbornly work with real, unpredictable and non-statistical children. They already knew that the brain is plastic. They started using developmental techniques with a few children, then with a full class room, and eventually with a whole school. First one school, then another and then still another! They are aware that today's children come to school – bright as a button - but often without those physical skills that are needed to ready the brain for academic success. They realize that today it should be the school's job, not just to teach, but to give the children the best brains needed to learn anything they want to do in later life.

These are the real heroes, the real movers and shakers that shape the world!

Svea J. Gold

Author of *If Kids Just Came with Instruction Sheets!*

Creating a World without Child Abuse: Fern Ridge Press, Oregon, U.S.A.

In consultation with
Louise Bates Ames Ph.D.   Carl H. Delacato, Ed.D.
Lendon H. Smith, M.D.   Ray C. Wunderlich Jr., M.D.
and many others

Contents

Chapter 7 – Learning Difficulty Support Groups 133

Children deserve all the support that Teachers and parents can get – whether the support comes from one person or a group. This chapter looks at a Learning Difficulties Support group, explaining its goals and function and giving advice on how to start one. We share experiences with starting an LD support group in Oxford Falls, Sydney, and also in Perth.

Chapter 8 – Research 143

We need good research to achieve the final step of getting basic movement sequences on the curriculum for all classrooms. Christine Chapparo tells of how she brought Occupational Therapy into 2 schools, and we share information about preparations for two exciting research programs that are currently underway.

Chapter 9 – Additional Resources 159

9a – Calming Overactivity in the classroom 161

Suggestions on how to calm the overactive and oversensitive children in a classroom by Occupational Therapist, Veronica Steer.

9b – Sound Therapy and Auditory Processing 167

Veronica Steer gives us an overview of the Sound Therapies available and what can be used as 'surround sound' in the home and classroom.

9c – Healing the Hurts 172

Learning Difficulties can cause deep hurts which often need healing. This chapter looks at various Healing Therapies that are available to relieve the stress caused by neurological, emotional and environmental imbalances.

Introduction

Introduction

Them his is one of those introductions that you don't want to miss. The first question I should be answering is why I am writing another book when it is such a hard thing to do. Haven't I already covered everything in the first three books?

The answer to that is no.

There is always more to learn, and new discoveries are being made every day. It seems, in fact, that the more we learn, the more questions become apparent, and since the writing of my first three books we have been flooded with questions, not just from those newly discovering the world of LD, but also from those who have been struggling with its issues for many years.

"How do I get your Movement Program into my school?"

"What do we do after your basic movement sequences?"

"The school doesn't think there is anything wrong with my child. To where can I turn?"

"Is crawling really that necessary?"

"I'm a single Mum and can't afford help. Is there anything I can do?"

"What are the symptoms of possible neurological immaturity in babies 0 to 3 years? Can you help me prevent problems before they really start?"

"I am a Teacher living in a country area in Mexico and no one around here can show me how to teach children who find it hard to learn. Can you help?"

"My child is never well, where can I find answers for this? Can you help me?"

"We need a *Support Group for Learning Difficulties* – how can I start one?"

"We live in Singapore and my son is in a highly achieving school and can't cope even though he is bright. Can you suggest anything?"

I couldn't answer all of these questions personally, but when necessary I knew who could. We located answers, or referrals to people **with** answers, and we sent off information to any who asked, but there was often far too much information to fit into a letter. With more and more questions coming in every day, we began to see the need for yet another book, one containing the answers to these commonly asked questions.

Nearly every second question was about how to make the Move to Learn program available and effective which in reality usually meant how do we get it into schools. This needed to be the main thrust of the book.

This book also details my various journeys in this whole field. First was my change from not being aware that we had a dyslexic child and even "What was that?", to the realization that a minimum of 20% of the world was struggling with the same basic challenge.

Then there was the journey from being proud of my clever little child who didn't even need to crawl to knowing that much of the world didn't know how important it was to crawl.

There was the maze we went through learning about the importance of what went into our stomachs and through our skin.

Research was a real turn around. We didn't want to have a bar of it for a long time because we didn't really know what specific thing to focus our research on, what view along the way that we really needed to look at in depth. And then arriving at a place where I am funding my own research.

We also had a kind of mystery tour when we didn't tell anyone what we were doing but during the journey we started to tell everyone we met.

The trip with our love/hate friend 'the computer', went from what can only be described as hate to knowing that he had to be with us because the Internet was the only way to go.

And then the view from the mountain at the end of the trip was seeing the movement sequences in every classroom of the world.

What a journey we have had!

Over the years that we have been investigating Learning Difficulties it has been significant and encouraging to notice who was asking these questions. Thirty five years ago nearly all of the questioners were parents. When I spoke at seminars twenty five years ago, even though Teachers were invited, the audience was almost entirely made up of parents, even at the night meetings. Thirty five years later it is now different. At least 25% of our enquirers are Teachers, and many people are recognizing that it is in school that children need to be helped to learn – it is not an extracurricular activity. The other interesting observation is that a number of Teachers are getting their students' parents to contact us. What a wonderful change!!!!!

It was the parents, however, who started the ball rolling. I have spoken to thousands of confused and hurting parents over the years – the finest group of desperate people you would ever want to meet. I had been one of them myself!

In so many cases, however, parents were looking to the school to help their child, as relatively few of the families could afford or find private help. Others somehow just couldn't get it together to use the help offered outside the school because they had other children to look after and other responsibilities, and many just had no idea what was really wrong in the first place.

Gradually, however, a variety of highly skilled and effective therapists and specialists have emerged and many of them are now aware of their role in helping LD students. Help is becoming more available and knowledge and understanding of the problem is spreading, meaning that we are now able to help about **1% of those needing it.**

But what about the 19% that remain?

That same niggling thought has been coming back to me for years. We surely don't have to just let them drift, be under-employed or unemployed, as well as part of the great majority of the residents of jails (goals). It is because of this 19% that I have written this book. **There is no way in the world these statistics need be so frightening when the answer is simple and inexpensive.**

Chapter 1

My Journey

Chapter 1

My Journey

When my bubbly, happy, whimsical, exceptionally inquisitive, ever talkative preschooler hopped over the threshold of school it was as if she had gone through C.S. Lewis' wardrobe and into a new land. Changes in her didn't happen overnight - but slowly and surely the butterfly became the worm. It took her a while to believe that she must be 'dumber' than her two friends, both named Cathie, but eventually she was sure of it. One sat on each side of her and they always got their hands up before her. Initially a ring leader, it only took three or so years before she fell into the pattern of walking around the playground by herself, kicking the small stones along the way.

The first day of kindergarten was particularly disappointing for her – she had wanted to learn to read that day.

Preschools were not common in Australia when my children were young, so they all had several eventful years to explore clay pits, fall down holes and get dirty. Nothing was impossible for them. If they didn't have something, they just pretended that they did, the only limit being their imagination - but when it came to sitting at a school desk, nearly everything became impossible for my little daughter. She couldn't sit still, and wasn't able to see the glary blackboard or copy accurately to her book. Not only did the *b's*, *p's* and *d's* change places but she was never sure whether the *b* was really a *b* or maybe a *d* or even a *q* or a *g*, because sometimes they tricked her.

At school, my perplexed, hurting little girl just kept quiet. I didn't know this because she was always expressing herself so abundantly at home. I waited nearly in vain for 'that phone call from the headmaster' summoning me to the school. How could Teachers run a classroom with my talkative daughter in it?

Over the whole of her schooling I was only called in twice. Once was at the end of grade two because she kept 'forgetting' to write all the numbers the right way round and had failed number work, and again, in grade four, when I was gently summoned in because the headmaster wondered if I could shed some light on why my daughter had so few friends.

Much damage was done to the spirit of that gorgeous little girl. Then again, several of my 9 grandchildren have had patches of very tough times, more than they deserved, and the problem is certainly not limited to my family or to the distant past. Thirty years on, we now have a variety of names and definitions of conditions that restrict our ability to learn, but knowing the names has not solved the problem. A horrifying minimum of 20% of the population is still affected significantly, and all we have really managed to do is to affect a limited kind of damage control for them. We are able to help some children **get around** their problems, but the vast majority are silently funnelled into underemployment, underachievement, poor self concept, drugs and jail (gaol). I thank God that my daughter had her pretend world already set in place before she went to school. She could escape there. It might have been a dark place at times but it offered shelter.

Near the end of our children's schooling I decided to go back to University to become a Teacher. I had my Bachelor of Arts from Winnipeg in Canada and needed an additional year to qualify as a High School Teacher. The Teacher's College I applied to here in

A Minimum of 20% Fall by the Wayside

Australia was not so impressed with my specialisation in Canadian History, but thought I could be a good Special Education Teacher because I was older. I wasn't sure that I would have the patience to cope with 'slow' children but that was the only alternative offered.

That year at College dramatically opened my eyes (as I explained in my first book) to the fact that some of my own family had Learning Difficulties, but I also knew that none of them were 'slow'. What's more, I learned that their difficulties were by no means unique. What surprised me the most, however, was the lack of real explanations or solutions to this problem. No one seemed to know **why** these children were struggling or how to help them.

Our Move to the Blue Mountains, New South Wales

After I had finished my studies, my husband and I moved up to the Blue Mountains to manage a motel that he had just built in Blackheath. I had always found it hard work to cater for my own family of five people, but at Redleaf Lodge Motel at first it was necessary for me to manage the dining room of a 60 bed conference motel. Even so I still wanted to make a start with my teaching, especially since I had been given such a new slant on our daughter's struggles at school.

One day I noticed an announcement in the Blue Mountains daily rag about a remedial reading class to be held every Thursday night in the community college in Katoomba. "Excellent", I thought. "I will go along tonight and ask the Teacher for permission to sit in on his class so I can see how he does it." I rolled up at 7pm, introduced myself to the registrar, and asked him if this would be possible.

As it turned out he was also the Teacher of the particular class that I wanted to view and he exclaimed, "How fortunate that you came. I am finding it difficult to be registrar and teach the class as well, so would you take over for just the first 10 minutes or so?"

"But what will I do? I haven't anything with me."

"You'll think of something", he said. "You've been to college."

So, in I went to the classroom, introduced myself and asked each one why they had come to this class and what they expected to get from it. Each story was totally different in this group of people from 16 to 60 years of age. "It's so good I don't have to teach such a diverse group of people like this!" I thought.

Well, Mr Registrar never showed his face and I had two hours of sudden improvised teaching. In fact he never ever showed his face on any of the following nights and finally after six weeks I started getting paid.

I realized very quickly that there was no way one person could effectively teach such a group of people with such different needs. Just at that time two other Teachers, Maxine Anderson and Trish Stevenson, happened to ask me to show them how I taught remedial work. So they came on staff also and we split my $20.00 nightly salary three ways.

With our 12 students, we three worked in 'stations'. Maxine taught phonetics and reading. Trish took each group through physical paces because I thought they all seemed very uncoordinated and I taught mathematics and anything else needed. But it still didn't seem to be enough. Several of the students needed more work in between classes, so I began teaching extra individual lessons for those who wanted them in the kitchen of our apartment at the motel.

With three Teachers and two hours every week the evening remedial class was growing, but progress was much quicker when the younger students came to the motel with their parents as well. Parental support doing daily reinforcement at home, even if it was only for 10 minutes or so, made all the difference.

This was the beginning of a journey that I have been travelling on ever since. In that small kitchen I tried to find answers to the puzzles each student presented but fortunately I haven't done this alone.

Many have walked this road with me; ahead, behind and beside. One of the dearest to me has been my long time companion and collaborator, Sister Yvonne Mary Ellis, an Our Lady of the Sacred Heart Convent nun who had taught in the Catholic School system for many years.

Walking with a Nun

I found Sister when I knocked on the door of the first convent I had ever approached. I had been knocking on many doors, (figuratively and literally), seeking advice, knowledge, and support. Sister had been recommended to me by Barbara Zaremba, Head of the Guild Centre Teachers' College in Sydney. She had just given a further education course on Learning Difficulties that Sister had attended, and she thought that sister would be perfect for me.

I had decided to advertise more broadly and hold a week long residential vacation program at our Motel for LD children and their parents, and I needed direction. I had heard so many accolades about Sister, and I set out to see if I could persuade her to help me. It wasn't as difficult as I'd expected. The conversation went something like this:

"Good afternoon, would you please tell me if there is a Sister Yvonne Mary here?"

"Yes, certainly. Just a minute please."

Footsteps behind the door.

"Yes, how can I help you?"

"Sister, my name is Barbara Pheloung. You were recommended to me by Barbara Zaremba. I need your help in running an in-house seminar for parents of children with Learning Difficulties and their children for a week at our motel."

"Certainly, when do we start?"

Sister and I on a Journey

Our First Venture Together

This was a residential vacation program for parents of children with LD and their children.

The emphasis of that first program was on parental involvement, education, movement and fun. Sister basically led the show and I followed her around absorbing information and supporting her where I could. We assessed each student, taught them phonics, did exercises, danced, painted and showed the parents what they needed to do after they got home. My friend, Maxine, from the evening college, taught swimming and my husband taught the children World War II marching to help with coordination, and my daughter ran drama classes. Everyone played a part, and the results were an enthusiastic success.

After the second of those highly intensive seminars, Sister and I worked as a team but in our own quarters. Sister worked near her convent in a part of a condemned building, (the part that wasn't condemned), and I continued in my kitchen. We still ran the remedial class at the night school, but our work was not fully understood by those who employed us and we were often referred to in humourous terms after they learned we used physical exercises to teach spelling.

People were being helped, however, and word got around about 'this Teacher, her helpers and the nun who all really helped kids'. The tiny motel kitchen got too crowded with all the home made equipment that our handyman at the motel, Perry Bottrell, and I had made. My husband built a whole new room on the back of our motel especially for me. It had a huge beautiful cupboard and an overhead ladder on the ceiling. I used the motel golf putting green and driving net as rewards for my good students, which actually included all of them.

The vision was taking shape.

Whenever I was stuck on how to help a student and thought I had tried everything, I would phone Sister for advice.

"Have you tried such and such?" she would answer in her gentle, excited way. "No? "Well, why don't you try that but don't tell anyone I said this."

We were both very unsure of ourselves in those days and we had many detractors.

It was generally thought that some people were just 'dumber' than the rest of us, but even our first tentative explorations and results convinced us that this was not the case. These children were often quite bright, **and** they were able to learn and improve.

They did, however, often need help beyond what we could offer in our special 'classrooms'. Many of the children showed evidence of underlying physical problems, and Sister and I began the search for appropriate professionals to refer them to. This proved more difficult than expected. We were able to find only three other professionals within a hundred kilometre radius – a Behavioural Optometrist, a Teacher of phonetics and a Doctor.

Travelling Around the Countryside

In some ways, as it turned out, it may have been part of the 'big plan' that there were so few resources in the Mountains because that forced us to learn as much as we could to fill in the gaps. We began travelling around the countryside, attending as many seminars as we could and soaking up knowledge at every opportunity from those who were already active in the field, such as Speech Therapists, Behavioural Optometrists, Educational Kinesiologists, Physiotherapists, Doctors, Audiologists, Occupational Therapists and Early Childhood Education Teachers. Fortunately my husband was relaxed about my travels with a nun, because he knew there would be no mischief.

Sister and I had just discovered rebounders at that time. They are a partial substitute for the best teaching aide of them all, the trampoline. The rebounder fitted into the back seat of my car and when we were tired from driving we would pull it out and each have a jump. Sister was a sight to behold with her habit fluttering up and down at the side of the road.

An unusual sight

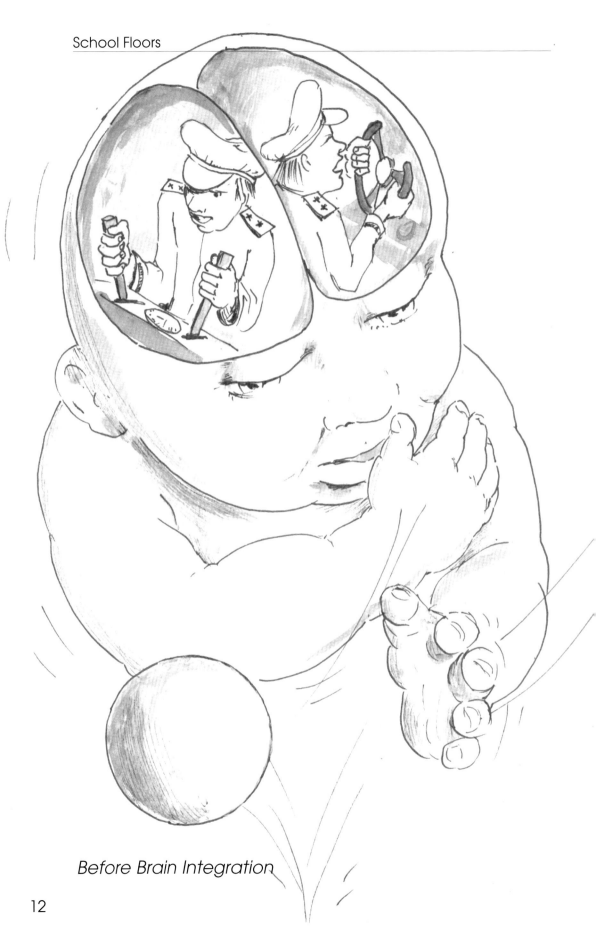

Before Brain Integration

Some of the most exciting seminars we attended were put on by ANSUA, *A New Start for the Underachiever*, in Sydney. Judy Tankard, a Physiotherapist, was the Director and she facilitated some wonderful input from pioneers like Dr. Mary Lou Sheil, Georgie Shaw, a resource Teacher, and Jill Taylor (King), a Paediatric Physiotherapist who was also a Feldenkrais Practitioner.

We also went to every single conference put on by Yvonne Stewart, who started and housed SPELD, *NSW Specific Learning Difficulties Association*. Yvonne was such an inspiration and help as she guided me, book by book, through SPELD's extensive library that filled her huge basement. "You must have this…and…oh..here is another excellent one by…." She would enthuse about every single book.

We asked many, many questions of Ken Johnson, Margaret Sasse, Jean Rigby, Maureen Hawke and Chris Henderson, and we soaked up books by Jean Ayres, Doman, Delacato, Tansley, Frostig, Wunderluck, Piaget, Kephart and Rob LeFroy.

There was so much to learn, and it was so helpful to be able to gain from the experience and knowledge of those who had gone before us and those who were working beside us. Each could provide a new insight, or a confirmation of our own or others' discoveries.

We learned about the importance of teaching phonics, investigated the whole area of nutrition, chemical imbalance, allergies and food intolerance and got all excited about the possibilities of a multi-sensory approach to education.

The progress of detectives Sister and Barb became a serial, and each episode revealed a new discovery, another cause for celebration, and another student who didn't have to struggle to learn anymore.

Then, patterns of clues began to emerge. One example was that not one of the victims of LD that I have seen in the last 32 years had the two sides of their brain working well together. None had what has been described as a 'well integrated brain'. The term 'brain integration' can be confusing because the word 'integration' can be used in several different ways. I always loved the way that the sisters, Margaret Sasse and Dr. Mary Lou Sheil, our guiding lights who pioneered this field in Australia, described integration of the brain.

Their picture of 'brain integration' went like this. When babies are born they act as if they have two separate brains because the paths between the left and right sides of the brain, through the corpus callosum, as babies, haven't yet developed very much. It is as though each side of the brain is being governed by its own general and each general is doing pretty much what he wants to do in isolation from the other. The result is that babies have little control over their limbs, eyes, etc, and one can go one way and the other another way.

One day, however, while they are on the floor, the generals manage to get their eyes to work together and they spot a bright red round thing just out of reach on the floor. One general says to the other, "How about we both get our hands to work together to get that bright thing over there? You put your hand under it and I'll put my hand over it, if I can?"

The other general replies "Sure thing, but you will have to raise your shoulder and arm. I'll put my shoulder and arm under my side."

"Hey, I think we might need to use our feet together as well, to do a little pushing. Do you know how to do that?"

It is in this way, through exploring and movement, that the two sides of the brain learn to 'talk' to each other via the corpus callosum. Gradually control improves and slowly one general proves to be a little stronger than the other, and, starts to take command of the whole body. The side of the body that he directly controls becomes the dominant or preferred side, and when he is fully in control you can say that the two halves of the brain are integrated. The body has decided which hand to write with, which foot to do the pushing on a scooter, which eye and which ear will be dominant, and **then** the child is ready for a desk and formal classroom learning. To attempt formal learning before full integration takes place, either before or after seven years of age, will usually result in frustration, struggle and often defeat.

It is true, however, that there are non-integrated children who do well in school **but** I have always wondered how much better they would have done if they hadn't had to use so much of the 'thinking' part of their brain to compensate for the 'automatic' part.

This explanation proved to be an invaluable one for us in our search for knowledge. The simple solution to a lack of integration, and the resulting Learning Difficulties it seemed to cause, proved to be to stimulate communication between the two halves of the brain through movement exercises. We found that by duplicating the natural activities through which this integration is normally gained in unimpaired individuals, (such as crawling, rolling, climbing, exploring), the blockages and paths through the corpus callosum could be cleared. Damage could be reversed because new brain cells can be built through movement and students could gain the integration they needed to enable them to learn.

Of course, many other factors can interfere with our ability to learn, including emotional and physical health, and each student must be looked at holistically. Quite often, more than one hindrance exists, and each must be dealt with for ultimate success, but one thing became clear:

In order to function at maximum capacity, we have to nourish our bodies in the way they were intended to be nourished and do much physical play and work.

Has this Always Been the Case?

When I was in Fiji a few years ago I talked with a Headmistress about our mutual concern for these children. A lady of my age, she had been around for a while, and had an interesting perspective to share.

"Years ago when I first started teaching on the islands," she said. "I can hardly remember anyone who didn't learn to at least read and write at school."

"They could **all** read and write?" I reacted in surprise.

"Oh yes", she said. "As well as that, the children spent most of their free time climbing coconut trees, swimming and going around on the rafts they had made themselves."

The Original Fijian's
Move to Learn

"What is different now?" I queried

"So many families have come to live in Suva, looking for work. Their children are sitting in overcrowded classrooms, in front of the TV at home and they get bussed to and from school."

To this mature Headmistress apparently the recent decrease in the children's activity seemed linked to the increased occurrence of Learning Difficulties.

In England, the story was similar. More and more children were struggling in school. The English answer had been to start teaching the children 'letter recognition' even earlier but the problem there was getting worse. Neither did the Australian 'solution' work, of cutting down on 'frills', such as dancing and music, so that more time could be spent looking at an open book. Cutting back on physical education and increasing book work didn't seem to be decreasing the number of struggling students.

We need to *move* to learn. Movement enables neurological development, but it has to be the right kind of movement and done in the appropriate order, the natural order of development. Each skill builds on the one just gained, to form a sound foundation. If you don't get the foundations solidly in place the building won't stand up, but it's simple to do this. Over the years of working with both children and adults with Learning Difficulties, we have developed an easily followed, correctly ordered movement program that has proven to be an effective means of increasing neurological maturity and integration.

Our Turn to Give Out

The more we learned the more we wanted to tell everybody else – whoever would listen, and after a while people began to ask. The message was beginning to filter out, and others, as desperate for information as we had been in the beginning, were seeking to network with us and share what we had discovered. Whenever any group of people would ask us to speak we always did so, no matter how small or remote the group. I did the public speaking and Sister did the private speaking. "As long as I don't have to get up and speak", she would say. She made the bullets and I fired them.

I won't recount here all the country towns in NSW we went to. They are the most welcoming warm places that anyone could ever want to visit. I'll never forget how they made us feel like royalty, even though I was nauseous and nervous. In utter disbelief I would be interviewed by the local television station, but it was such fun doing it!

The Visiting Celebrity

Soon it became clear, however, that we couldn't visit everywhere. There had to be a better way to reach more people. Barry, my husband finally came up with the solution.

He bought me a little Apple Computer and put it on my desk. "You are only helping 20 families a year now. You will have to write up what you have learned so more people can benefit, and it doesn't just apply to the strugglers. Your book will be one that every parent and Teacher can use."

Writing this first book, *Help Your Child to Learn* was the hardest road I had ever travelled but Sister, God bless her, helped hugely all the way, and the book was well received and **did** manage to bring our message to many that we would never have been able to reach face to face.

The Next Step

After nine years in the Blue Mountains my husband and I needed to move back to Sydney and the opportunity arose for us to purchase a very long narrow house right on Manly Beach. The idea was to set up a place in the community where children with LD could be brought for help from Teachers and Physical Therapists at minimum cost using my mostly homemade equipment. This had to be brought down from the Blue Mountains and the hardest one to move was my overhead ladder that had been attached parallel to the ceiling of my teaching room. But we got the ladder and everything else moved into the garage and the rooms of the Beach House. The trampoline fitted into what became my work room with its high old ornate ceiling.

Sister had also been moved down to the Sydney convent in Kensington, where she had been set up with her own teaching quarters. We were able to visit often and share the excitement of each of us having such beautiful places to work from.

So we were part of the big city.

Sister continued to work alone, but I gathered a number of other professionals to work jointly with me, including Jill Taylor (King). She was an immensely helpful mate in this project. She blessed us with her wonderful knowledge of child development and had the perfect skills to complement the other wonderful Teachers, Occupational Therapists and Physiotherapists who also joined us.

The main purpose of the Beach House was to see how such a learning centre would work. In a sense, we hoped that we could develop a prototype, get the bugs out of it, document its successes and then write about it to empower and encourage any group of Teachers, therapists and parents to do the same in any old garage and in any town. This part of the journey inspired our next book, *Overcoming Learning Difficulties*, which I wrote together with Jill Taylor (King).

The Beach House **did** work well, and hundreds of children were helped. More excitingly, I've heard of a number of duplications that have proved equally successful. Julia Dive, an exceptionally dedicated Teachers' aide has been gracious enough to share her back garage experience with us later in the book. But hers is a Green Shed. I hope there are many other back garages and green sheds elsewhere.

Networking In The Big City

Now that we were based in Sydney, we were able to hook up more closely with a lot of the precious people who had supported us from afar when we began in the mountains. Mary Lou Sheil, on one of my visits to her home in Hunters Hill, said to me, "We now need to meet together more often to learn from each other, Barb. You start a group because I am too busy. But we can meet here."

So, PHLD, *Professional Help for Learning Difficulties*, was born. We met regularly in our homes, attracting many different professionals with a common concern to help those with Learning Difficulties.

The Beach House also became a centre of dissemination. We often had visiting professionals of every description meet with us in our staff meetings. These meetings became vibrant, unorthodox sessions of sharing, searching, exchanging and discussing new information as we sat around a table together eating our own paper bag lunches.

Into the Schools

It became more and more obvious that to help all of our needy children we needed to run these programs in **every** school. Even if there were hundreds of Julia Dives, and hundreds of 'Beach Houses' and 'Green Sheds', we would never be able to reach all of the struggling 20%, but how could we do this?

The first step was to get into a school myself, so that we could learn.

In 1991 I heard that Oxford Falls Grammar School in Sydney was looking for a remedial Teacher. My husband literally ear-bashed me into applying to the school. This was a good school with a very open-minded headmaster, Andrew Egan, who had a big heart for disadvantaged kids. He was willing to allow me to incorporate our movement programs into the academic timetables of kindergarten to year six, but it took a year before an appropriate space could be found for our work. We spent the first five months at the back of the canteen in a space two metres by three metres, but eventually we progressed to a portable classroom, where the program officially started in 1992, and finally into an old house. Robyn Taylor, a wonderful Educational, Clinical Psychologist who wanted to finish her *Study of Sensory Integration combined with Remedial Teaching Methods*, joined with me to do her research, help with the assessments and also oversee and plan the program for each child.

I will always be grateful for the opportunity that I was given. It was a wonderful 28 months' experience that confirmed, to our excitement, that this was indeed the way to go. Parents loved it, dozens of children's lives were changed and Robyn's research now lives at the back of *Help Your Class to Learn*, my third book, published in 1997.

The DVD

The more work we did, the more children that were helped, the further our message and methods seemed to spread and we received more and more requests for seminars. I was always happy to do these. It was so exciting to see people come alive with hope and then to hear back later of their successes, but in the early 1990s my husband's health was beginning to fail and I became hesitant to leave him alone.

My daughter finally came up with a solution. She suggested that we make a video that covered the information I would normally present in my seminars so that **it** could travel instead of **me**. This seemed like a great idea. We had never made an educational video before, but my daughter took on the task and produced the video *Help your Child to Learn* in 1993 with a handheld camera and a bed light. The sound quality wasn't the best, but it met the need for a while.

Soon, however, we were getting other requests. My third book, *Help Your Class To Learn* was published in 1997 and people were wanting to be coached through the movement programs described within. As with all learning, a multi-sensory approach is more effective. Groups found it easier if they could **see** the exercises demonstrated as well as **hear** a verbal commentary. This is where the idea came for our second video *Move to Learn*. Once again, my daughter jumped on board to help fulfil yet another of her mother's 'crazy visions', but this time we found the money to add to the production values and ensure professional sound and lighting quality.

This DVD is now a standard inclusion in our program and is playing a vital role in bringing movement programs into the schools.

Up to Date

And so that brings you up to date, as I sit here and write yet another 'Final Book'. It's been a long journey, and it's not over yet. I hope that it will not be over until every child in every school is receiving the help that they need to learn to their true potential.

Chapter 2

Climbing the Pyramid

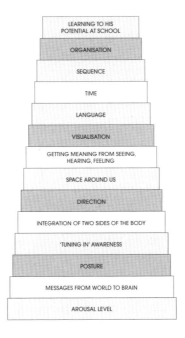

LEARNING TO HIS
POTENTIAL AT SCHOOL

ORGANISATION

SEQUENCE

TIME

LANGUAGE

VISUALISATION

GETTING MEANING FROM SEEING,
HEARING, FEELING

SPACE AROUND US

DIRECTION

INTEGRATION OF TWO SIDES OF THE BODY

'TUNING IN' AWARENESS

POSTURE

MESSAGES FROM WORLD TO BRAIN

AROUSAL LEVEL

Chapter 2

Climbing the Pyramid

The Birth of the Pyramid

When my pyramid was first born I could not claim parenthood because it was originally conceived by someone else. It was so long ago that I cannot even remember who its real parents were. But that is how things like pyramids are born – a little bit like illegitimate children. In actual fact illegitimacy is okay because that is how my whole vision has come about – all of us using other people's ideas and building on them. And that is what I am – a good brain picker. I have always worked with a select group of others who have the same love for 'strugglers' that I do and also the same transparency and willingness to share discoveries made and lessons learned.

The pyramid was born out of need because we wanted a way to illustrate the importance of foundational, pre-school learning. Our ideas weren't really new but they certainly weren't being taught in Teachers' colleges or practiced in most schools and we needed to be able to make a strong, clear statement of what we believed.

In my search for a way to do this I had come across one or two 'ladders of learning'. These were simple diagrams, based on the structure of a ladder, that illustrated the importance of priorities and of taking one step at a time to climb closer to a determined goal. Simple, initial skills would be listed at the bottom of the ladder and more complex ones up at the top with appropriate transition skills in between. The idea is that with learning a skill, as in climbing a ladder, you need to do it one step at a time, and in the right order. You need to understand the concept of a number, for instance, before you can learn to add or subtract.

Ladders, therefore, illustrated the process of learning well because they explained how we have to climb up from the bottom. We have to go through the steps of becoming 'ready to learn' before we can achieve academic success.

But I also wanted to illustrate the importance of firm foundations, of how each acquired skill builds on skills previously acquired and lays the base for the next level of learning or development. 'Pyramids' seemed to fill the bill. Without really strong foundations all in place, the top of a pyramid would either collapse or be wobbly.

We found that a pyramid illustrating normal neurological development was particularly useful in our work with children who struggled with difficulties in reading, writing, spelling and mathematics. Often such a child could be identified as having incomplete or immature

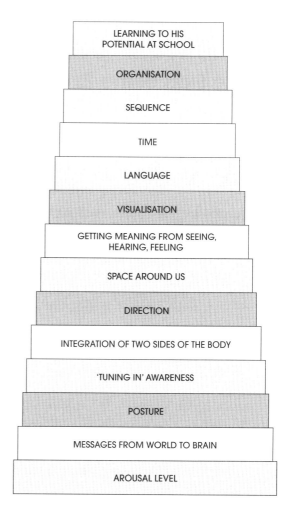

LEARNING TO HIS POTENTIAL AT SCHOOL

ORGANISATION

SEQUENCE

TIME

LANGUAGE

VISUALISATION

GETTING MEANING FROM SEEING, HEARING, FEELING

SPACE AROUND US

DIRECTION

INTEGRATION OF TWO SIDES OF THE BODY

'TUNING IN' AWARENESS

POSTURE

MESSAGES FROM WORLD TO BRAIN

AROUSAL LEVEL

neurological development and by looking for the immature areas in each child's development, and then comparing this with normal neurological growth on the pyramid, we were able to locate and work on these areas of immaturity in the correct order. The pyramid diagram provided an easily used and understood reference tool.

The Symptoms of Immaturity Added

It is interesting to watch how my 'pyramid' has changed over the years and grown in usefulness. As I travelled around it started to become obvious how helpful it would be to briefly describe the symptoms of immaturity for each stage of development so that parents could visualise without having to read a book as to where the difficulties of each of their children were on the ladder. For example, some of the common symptoms of 'poor integration of the two sides of the body' (not automatically knowing their right hand from their left, reversing letters and struggling) were written on the Pyramid.

This diagram can be found in *Help Your Class to Learn*, which was designed to go with the DVD/video, and the explanation of the Pyramid is on pages 26ff. It has also been reproduced over the page.

Jill's Pyramid of Learning

In our book, *Overcoming Learning Difficulties* (p. 75) Jill provided us with her own Pyramid of Learning which has big stone blocks to demonstrate the need for a strong foundation. She often used this pyramid as she talked to her students' parents. From that illustration parents could easily see what building blocks were missing in their children. For example, if the 'touch' foundation was immature, parents could look up all the tactile activities that they could do at home.

The questions in that particular book are a more detailed list of symptoms of immaturities and those questions are now used by many professionals including Psychologists and Occupational Therapists.

The Pyramid and the Brain

When Veronica and I were planning *School Floors* she wrote about

THE LADDER OF LEARNING

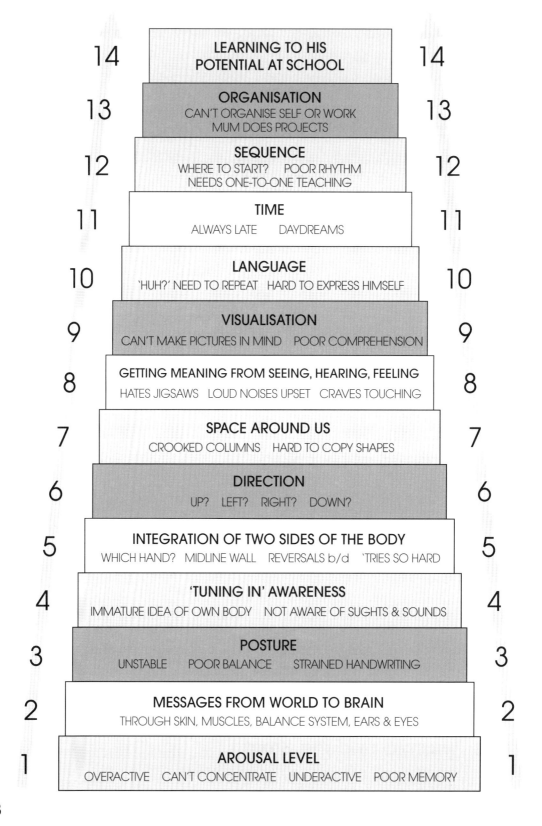

14 — LEARNING TO HIS POTENTIAL AT SCHOOL — 14

13 — **ORGANISATION**
CAN'T ORGANISE SELF OR WORK
MUM DOES PROJECTS — 13

12 — **SEQUENCE**
WHERE TO START?   POOR RHYTHM
NEEDS ONE-TO-ONE TEACHING — 12

11 — **TIME**
ALWAYS LATE   DAYDREAMS — 11

10 — **LANGUAGE**
'HUH?' NEED TO REPEAT   HARD TO EXPRESS HIMSELF — 10

9 — **VISUALISATION**
CAN'T MAKE PICTURES IN MIND   POOR COMPREHENSION — 9

8 — GETTING MEANING FROM SEEING, HEARING, FEELING
HATES JIGSAWS   LOUD NOISES UPSET   CRAVES TOUCHING — 8

7 — **SPACE AROUND US**
CROOKED COLUMNS   HARD TO COPY SHAPES — 7

6 — **DIRECTION**
UP?   LEFT?   RIGHT?   DOWN? — 6

5 — INTEGRATION OF TWO SIDES OF THE BODY
WHICH HAND?   MIDLINE WALL   REVERSALS b/d   'TRIES SO HARD — 5

4 — **'TUNING IN' AWARENESS**
IMMATURE IDEA OF OWN BODY   NOT AWARE OF SUGHTS & SOUNDS — 4

3 — **POSTURE**
UNSTABLE   POOR BALANCE   STRAINED HANDWRITING — 3

2 — MESSAGES FROM WORLD TO BRAIN
THROUGH SKIN, MUSCLES, BALANCE SYSTEM, EARS & EYES — 2

1 — **AROUSAL LEVEL**
OVERACTIVE   CAN'T CONCENTRATE   UNDERACTIVE   POOR MEMORY — 1

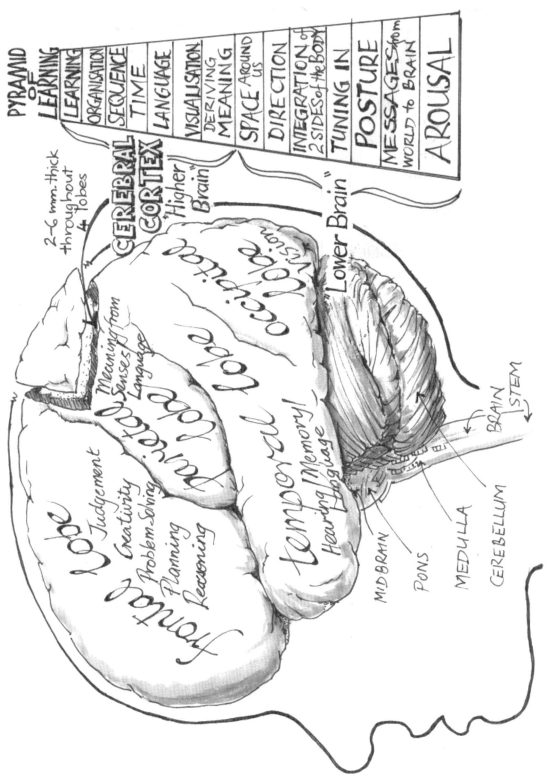

The following text appears within the illustration:

PYRAMID OF LEARNING		
LEARNING		
ORGANISATION		
SEQUENCE		
TIME		
LANGUAGE		
VISUALISATION		
DERIVING MEANING		
SPACE AROUND US		
DIRECTION		
INTEGRATION of 2 SIDES of the BODY		
TUNING IN		
POSTURE		
MESSAGES from WORLD to BRAIN		
AROUSAL		

2-6 mm. thick throughout 4 lobes

CEREBRAL CORTEX "Higher Brain"

"Lower Brain"

occipital lobe

Vision

frontal lobe
Judgement
Creativity
Problem-Solving
Planning
Reasoning

parietal lobe
Meaning from Senses
Language

temporal lobe
Hearing Memory Language

BRAIN STEM

MID BRAIN
PONS
MEDULLA
CEREBELLUM

The Pyramid of Learning and the Brain

the brain and about which activities helped mature which parts of the brain. She conceived this clever illustration, which was then executed by my illustrator, Tony, with the pyramid beside a drawing of the brain, showing what areas of the brain are matured by the movement sequences.

Using the Pyramid as a Record of Achievement

A further use for the Pyramid popped into my cortex while we were setting up the LD Support group. We could use it to record the needs of each student, see where therapy needed to start and then as each immature area was addressed it could be ticked off. For example when the lowest level, the whole area of food intolerance and chemical imbalance was investigated and the student either did not have problems there or they had been successfully identified and at least started to be addressed that bottom row could have a tick or a line through it. Other areas of development could be marked the same way if there was no apparent immaturity so that parents and Teachers could see at a glance what needed attention next. It also became a record of what had been done.

'Assessment' is Seldom Necessary or Useful

When a child presents with Learning Difficulties it is often suggested that a full academic/psychological assessment be made to determine fully where the student's problems lie. This pyramid won't provide this, but in actual fact a full academic/psychological assessment is only needed if a family is applying for funding. We have also found that, apart from the fact that they can be expensive and potentially damaging to a child's self-esteem, a full assessment is not even really useful because the whole picture of the child can change once foundational immaturities are addressed. For instance, if food intolerance is found to be a factor for a child's difficulty, when that is normalised their academic performance can dramatically improve. On a number of occasions I have also seen remarkable language improvements, as well as handwriting improvements after only six weeks of daily 10 minute trampolining sessions.

Chapter 3

An Occupational Therapist on the Same Road

Chapter 3

An Occupational Therapist on the Same Road

(My Story, as told by Veronica Steer, Occupational Therapist in Adelaide, Australia)

When I received a phone call from Barbara asking if I would like to join her for her *Move to Learn Seminar* in 2004, as the Occupational Therapist on her team, I was overwhelmed and wondered if I was the right person. I didn't live in Sydney, and I hadn't worked with Barbara before. In fact we hadn't even met each other. I was using the book *Overcoming Learning Difficulties* in my work, and a colleague of Barbara's, Dr. Marilyn Dyson, had suggested that I might 'fit the job'.

I have always accepted invitations to talk to Teachers, parents and other professionals so I very humbly and eagerly accepted, and hoped I had the knowledge for which she was looking.

"Hello Sydney! Barbara, here I come." As I got off the ferry to meet Barbara for the first time in 2003 I was very well aware that here I was in Sydney again, dear Sydney. Not only had I been influenced by my mother and father's love of Sydney from working here during the war, but it had been the biggest influence in my professional life.

As an undergraduate in the '70s I elected to finish my clinical requirements at the Royal Prince Alfred Hospital and Mosman

Spastic Centre. I did little in the hospital, as I and my fellow Adelaide students were whisked away to a two week 'camp' at Hunters Hill. This was a summer school called *Threshold* established by a Psychologist and a Behavioural Optometrist and assisted by many LD workers including one of the first OTs in Australia to use *Sensory Integration Therapy*. It was wonderful to see children being engaged in such a combination of 'getting the body right' to serve the special education support that was provided.

I then attended the Mosman Spastic Centre where OTs sat with children in wheelchairs and taught an intellectual approach to distance, height, spacing, numbers, letters and writing. No! This did not seem right! What about children getting to know their bodies on the floor, finding out about their fingers and body space? Where was the movement and the body in relation to this intellectual learning?

Back in Adelaide I was greatly privileged to work at the Spastic Centre there, and, to be given a 'free hand' to set up trampolines, hammocks, scooter boards, rugs, barrels and tactile boxes, for children to swing, bounce, to lie on, in, under, feel and explore. Engaging the whole child in their learning through their body and having fun at the same time was what we were able to provide in therapy.

One of my role models and a great encourager for families and workers at the Centre at that time was Dr. Susan Beal, originally a Sydneysider herself who later made the breakthrough discovery of the high incidence of *Sudden Infant Death Syndrome* in children who slept on their tummies. This finding has revolutionised the statistics worldwide of this heartbreaking cause of infant death by educating parents to limit the causes of suffocation: loose bedding and tummy sleeping. Babies can get plenty of 'tummy work' on the floor.

It was with Susan's family, who lived in Sydney, where I stayed to do my extra practical training in assessment together with the latest ways of helping children with all ranges of neurological impairment, particularly *Sensory Integration Therapy*, with Dr. Chris Chapparo, an enormous supporter, teacher and inspiration for many therapists in Australia and overseas. More recently I have been able to learn about *Sound Therapy*. What a wonderful addition *Sound Therapy* has been in helping with listening and remembering, talking and ease in working with concepts for children and adults. And I have taken a number of courses in kinesiology.

So here I was on the Manly Wharf waiting to meet this Barbara Pheloung. Oh, she was so lovely! Engaging and gentle. Clear and strong in where she was heading.

But what did we have in common? A great deal as it turned out, and it was so encouraging that our experiences and commitment to our work complemented each other in so many ways.

Friends

We were 'preaching' a similar message to help children learn but had arrived at the same understanding from different beginnings: Barbara from experience to theory, and me from theory to experience.

Our common beliefs included a commitment to the role of movement in learning, developing foundations first and educating parents and Teachers in practical ways of helping students with LD.

My occupational therapy background gave me strong basics in the brain and also in therapy to stimulate brain development, *Sensory Integration Therapy*, as developed by Dr. A. Jean Ayres in the '60s, '70s and '80s. She was a wonderful person, and an Occupational Therapist well ahead of her time, who was committed to developing a therapy and assessment with a neuroscience and research base. She believed in respecting and working at each individual child's level – getting down onto the floor, developing and following their drive, sense of challenge, fun and ensuring success and self worth.

In simple terms, Ayres recognised that many children's learning and behaviour difficulties were connected with using their body senses inefficiently – i.e. body movement, balance and gravity sense, body awareness sense, and the sense of touch, etc. These sensory systems not only form foundations for mastery, security and physical, emotional, and social interactions but also contribute to important perceptions of experience that help more abstract thinking and perception. In doing so they establish stronger lower brain processing to serve higher processing for language and classroom learning. Immature movement patterns and postures have to be integrated to allow for more mature balance and eye-hand and bilateral body activities as they also reflect poorly established lower brain function.

My work with this therapy started with children with cerebral palsy, continued with children with Learning Difficulties at a general hospital and later with children with severe and multiple disabilities. Repeatedly I set up therapy rooms in old houses, empty hospital wards waiting for funding to be commissioned, or the off times at the chapel and made many friends with the maintenance men who were cajoled into suspending hammocks, making 'flying saucers' and 'kangaroo swings'.

It was the experience with children with severe and multiple disabilities that convinced me that by providing movement, touch and muscle work stimulation in a structured, developmentally relevant, enjoyable and motivating way, children 'came alive'. They responded to their therapy, home, play and learning challenges in a more effective way. Life for these children became easier, in all their environments. Parents saw some of the biggest gains in ease of living in their children. Teachers saw happier, more motivated and settled students. They were more ready to deal with the learning or language challenges and interventions in which they were involved.

I later set up *Occupational Therapy for Children in Adelaide* in a cottage in the city. I was my own boss and able to provide this type of intervention for children to a standard that could be set between the parents and myself – not set by other management. It was based on gaining an understanding of children in various aspects of their development and daily life. We used appropriate assessment and therapy tools to assist their mastery in life – the basic tenet of occupational therapy. Over the 15 years of running this practice I had the privilege of working with 10 wonderful therapists who loved the children and their families and saw the importance of getting down and getting dirty. Being able to work barefooted with the kids all day was a bonus.

It was so rewarding to teach parents and Teachers some 'day to day hints'. With a little knowledge of the types of sensory based behaviour, and a little about brain processing, they were able to observe children, work out which sensory system or systems were immature, and help their ability to settle, to attend, to improve their behaviour, coordination and learning in the classroom, school yard and at home. More of the activities they were seeking (or rejecting) were incorporated : e.g. 'the fidgeter', was given items with which to fiddle, 'the tigger' was given bouncing, jumping and rolling activities, and the 'the mouther' was given items to suck, swallow, chew and blow.

Things to fiddle with

To read Barbara's and Jill Taylor's (King) book, *Overcoming Learning Difficulties* was awe-inspiring. It incorporated multiple and multi-disciplinary teaching and therapy strategies for home and school. Parents we worked with loved it. The OT's used many of the ideas in therapy as children's sensory and physical systems matured and recommended activities to help parents with their children at home.

Barbara and her husband's experience of their daughter's apparent brightness but nightmarish school experiences gave Barbara her commitment to understand and help others like their daughter as much as possible. She read and read and read, attended many workshops, visited many professionals and used what worked. She went back to University to learn more and then found she was in a position to help other children. She also found out that her 'work' and enquiries went far beyond what was being taught to special education trainee Teachers.

Barbara, with Sister Yvonne, Jill Taylor (King) and countless others and with the support of her husband Barry, finessed and further developed an effective, practical and 'cheap' way to get children learning better, starting with movement and body work.

The *Move to Learn* Sequences now epitomise Barbara's passion: help as many children as possible, in the most accessible and practical low cost way and where they happen - at school. These sequences are done by the Teachers with the whole class at school, with no extra equipment other than the floor and DVD/video, for short periods daily, with breakthrough results for most. They are based on how children's neurological development occurs, how bodies learn about themselves and the world around: by being in contact with the ground, holding up against gravity, rolling, crawling, and walking. These movement sequences also help integrate primitive movement patterns or reflexes. Amazingly simple!

Since Jean Ayres's early findings, there continues to be growing **research** that movement and bodywork improve **brain function** and learning. It appears to relieve stress and help with motivation as well as coordination, to which Barbara expresses gleefully that she knew their work worked, but now knows **why**. With the right stimulation, new brain cells can develop, especially in the part of the brain that is involved in memory, and movement is the essential component of the enriched environment. Integration of early primitive reflexes is necessary to free the brain processing for academic learning. **The *Move to Learn* Sequences are the essence or bare bones that will kick-start people with Learning Difficulties and enable them to learn academically and socially** -as Barbara continually says.

So Barbara and Sydney, I'm all yours!
Just call and I'll be there and share what I can.

Chapter 4

Feeding the Brain

Chapter 4

Feeding the Brain

E very day on the news there is concern expressed about the effects of our Western lifestyle on our children - 'obesity', 'empty calories', 'repeated series of infections', 'allergies', 'under-active couch-sitters' but also 'children who can't sit still'.

We are learning, however, that there is a great deal we can do to intervene for our families. Let me take one example: just the other day we heard about the outstanding improvement in an autistic child's ability to learn because of a significant increase in Omega 3 based linseed supplement. This child could not tolerate fish oil but could utilize this vegetable oil. His mother, family and friends noted a remarkable difference in language, both speaking and comprehending, and this has benefited all aspects of his life.

Then there is the simple long held, but often forgotten knowledge of the importance of eating enough protein. While I was at Oxford Falls Grammar School, I used to arrive before school started and take several students, one at a time, through the trampoline sequences. One of the boys would sometimes arrive having had no breakfast or only a serving of sugar laden breakfast cereal. It was useless for us to spend time on the trampoline those mornings because he had no concentration to do what he normally loved.

"Have some protein for breakfast tomorrow, Rod, and I'll see you then", I would say.

Sweden overcomes this problem by feeding all children a hot lunch high in fish and low in sugar. Protein meets the need for the body's growth and keeps the energy release from the food at a steady rate over the day. Fish has Omega 3 oil in it and any harm done by white sugar is addressed.

In order to learn, you have to have a well functioning brain. We have to stop kidding ourselves that junk food is good enough for our children. Research shows that there is an alarmingly high level of fat and starch and a lack of nourishment in a large proportion of take-away food. We are crippling our children with junk food!

Waiting for their turn on the trampoline

Over-sensitivity

There is, however, more to the food story than just the lack of concentration and over or under activity. There is the whole spectrum of over-sensitivity in children and adults.

• Do you notice people with eye shades and dark glasses inside buildings which have glary over-head lights?

• Do you see people 'drifting off' at meetings and lectures even though you know they are interested in what is going on? When I give a seminar and someone's head occasionally nods I choose to believe they are not bored but that they have poor auditory processing (ability to listen).

One in the Audience has Auditory Processing Problems

• Do you remember being critical of parents who appeared to be catering to the food tastes of their 'fussy eater'? You may not have known about food sensitivities and food intolerance. When I was young most children could eat everything that Mum bought and cooked. Nowadays, there have been so many additives and preservatives put into our foods that these chemicals are reducing the function of our nervous systems. Research suggests that some children's 'fussiness' is actually grounded in common sense. Their stomachs know what things don't react well with their bodies.

• Do you feel annoyed when it appears that some parents can't control their child or stop temper tantrums even in their older children? Chemical additives to our foods can contribute to this problem.

• Do any of you feel you are losing your memory at too young an age? Processed food with additives can be at least part of the problem.

• Do any of you wonder why all these problems seem to be getting dramatically worse? New additives are added to our foods every year.

This hurts more than her pride

• The number of vaccinations our children are subjected to increases all the time. Research suggests that the mercury from these vaccinations can build up in our bodies and poison us. It is also dangerous to give more than one vaccination at a time. For some people, giving more than one vaccination at a time can severely stress their immune systems and trigger other problems like Autism.

• More and more children and adults have been given antibiotics. The over-use of antibiotics can lead to 'a leaky gut' which means we don't absorb nutrients efficiently and then learning becomes harder.

• And do you wonder why there seem to be children who catch everything and are never really well? Food can certainly be related to this.

• And what about those who have ear infection after ear infection? If this is happening while they are learning to speak it usually slows down their development of speech and often their reading. Many parents, nutritionists and doctors believe that the need for grommets can be connected to the intake of dairy products.

My Journey with Nutrition

Nutrition first interested me when our son, as a teenager, took himself off to a naturopath for help with his asthma. He came back home that afternoon as a vegetarian. The family reaction was interesting. My husband announced that he was going to continue to eat meat and junk food. Our youngest said that she was going to stick with Dad. Our other daughter said she would keep her brother company and become a vegetarian. And I became a bit of both. The change, thankfully, made a huge difference to our son who had had asthma since the age of five.

Parents and Associates Taught me a Lot

The next big impact on me of the importance of the right diet came

Each to his own taste

when I started my work in the field of Learning Difficulties, and here Dr. Mary Lou Sheil was a constant source of inspiration and information. On the other end of the phone I could often be found desperately trying to keep up with her quick brain as I devised short-hand symbols to take notes as she spilled out pearls of hard won wisdom regarding nutrition, chemical imbalance and poisoning, allergies and food intolerance.

Parents and associates also taught me a lot. The first child I saw whose parents took him off all white sugar, had radically improved concentration in a few days. After a long time of working with her, one of my first Sydney students at the Beach House was finally released to learn to her potential after eliminating beans from her diet. There were many examples of dairy products linking up to ear infections and wheat linking with over-activity. The list goes on and on. Half of the children who came to us at the Beach House for help with reading, spelling, handwriting and mathematics were prone to glue ear and nasal problems. (This was shown up in a study done at the Beach House of 187 students in the early 1990s and recorded in *Help Your Class to Learn*, Pages 114/5, if the reader cares to look it up).

It's So Hard to Change your Diet

Food is a huge part of our everyday life – especially if we feel 'down' it can be a real comfort. To eliminate some of the foods we really like to eat can result in us feeling deprived. My efforts at giving up coffee were classic. I used to drink so much of it that I would literally 'shake' on occasions. Once I faced the fact that there was a connection between excessive caffeine and the 'shakes' it wasn't too hard to cut down. No more than three cups a day, unless I was celebrating. The next few years saw me experimenting with a number of levels of consumption. I eliminated it altogether a few times, and then cut it back to two a day, unless I was celebrating. An article declaring that coffee was actually beneficial for some people let me right off the hook for a while, because I was certainly a member of the 'some people'. Then decaffeinated and finally organic coffee appeared. That period of blissful indulgence didn't last however. My body continued to protest and I cut back to one organic coffee a day, but even then I was eventually confronted with a decision. Coffee or organic red wine – but not both. There was no way I was giving up my wine!

The physical benefits of this decision have encouraged me to accept and mostly persevere with this deprivation, but I must admit that I still feel the pull when I smell that beautiful coffee aroma.

My friends have other addictions. One of them loved and ate large amounts of cheese and then found that she could no longer tolerate dairy foods. My husband loved chocolates and used to hide them from the rest of us when he was given a box as a gift.

We often seem to love the foods we are accustomed to. Wouldn't it be wonderful to have been part of a family that had accustomed you to the food that was actually good for each member? To change your diet mid-stream can be an overwhelming task, especially at times when you are needing a bit of extra comfort.

An empty box of chocolates

How to Change our Food Habits

'Doing something is better than doing nothing' was Sister's favourite saying.

- Maybe, **a bit at a time**. It is amazing how much good can be achieved by making even **one** change to a family's eating habits.

"Let's drink water instead of a fizzy drink for 5 days a week for a period of time."

"Let's just drink a lot more water". One classroom Teacher told me that the fluid levels of children in her class were really low. Some of her students didn't drink anything all the time they were in school – not even a fizzy drink. She now encourages them all to bring a bottle of water from home each day.

"How about we read labels and eliminate two foods with additives in them?"

- Become aware of what you actually are eating by doing a food journal, listing everything you eat and drink for around five days.

The same Teacher, mentioned above, asked her students to write down everything they ate and drank for a school week. Some of them got help from home to do this. One of the children in the class had been away when she originally talked to the class about doing this. So this student was only told on the Monday morning that they had started to do it. It was interesting for the Teacher to see the child's journal at the end of the week. The first day was just junk food but this radically changed for the rest of the week.

Several examples of these food journals are at the back of the book in Chapter 9d, *Additional Resources*.

• Get educated. The subject of nutrition can be very confusing, with multiple 'experts' touting different theories of what is good for you and what is not. There appear to be some universal principles, but there are also individual cases where what is right for one person may not be the best for another. The solution is to discover what is right for you and those you love. A list of questions dealing with identifying nutritional problems can be found on page 63/4 in *'Help Your Child to Learn'*, for anyone to use, and the advice of a trusted nutritionist and/or naturopath is often a good place to start. A list of recommended reading can also be found at the end of this chapter.

• It helps if 'everyone else is doing it'. Protect your family by hiding your chocolates from them. Conspire with other parents before planning the food for picnics and parties. It also takes away peer pressure in schools if tuck shops do not stock foods that have a bad effect on children's behaviour, learning and health.

• Never tell husbands or children that certain foods 'are good for them' until they express an interest. Nagging never works. Just look after yourself and your example of lots of energy, practically no colds or flu, good looks and sex appeal will inspire others to copy you.

• You can assure yourself that deprivation won't go on forever. This was how I gave up smoking. I promised myself that when I got into a nursing home I would smoke as much as I wanted - five packs a day, if I so desired.

I will smoke as much as I want

• I also made myself indignantly angry at the thought of money-making magnates running **my** family's life. How dare they decide what they were going to sneak into our foods without us knowing! We should all have a chance to be vigorous enough to make love at a ripe old age if it's appropriate.

I don't want to need someone to look after me because of ill health that is not necessary. To get really angry all I have to do is to start to read food labels and learn what the many unnecessary additives actually are and what they are doing to everyone's health.

• And we all can do with a dose of support from others. Two very special naturopaths helped me through the experience of fighting cancer and then with generating enough energy to go back to write this book and tell the world that we can overcome LD and almost everything else – but we also need healthful, simple food and lots of exercise.

It's Cool to Eat Smart

Teachers can join with parents in encouraging children to put the right things into their stomachs. I'm not suggesting that Teachers have time to think about their student's food intake but the best teaching in the world will be to no avail if the children have had no protein for breakfast or eat loads of food with additives and junk food.

I remember so many things my favourite Teachers said, and I'm positive that if they had said more about good nutrition, I would have wanted to eat better – especially if they had told me it would have helped my basketball.

Nowadays we are actually in the middle of a war. Us against the companies who change our beautiful food by processing and putting additives and chemicals in so much of it by adding false colour, stronger flavour and preservatives that extend shelf life to sell more. We are having to fight for our lives. It's usually a slow, insidious death and hard to detect until the time comes when too much damage has already been done to our minds and bodies when we finally decide to change things.

Parents and Teachers are on the same side of this battle for a good healthy long life for our children. Teachers can help so much to change the diet from it being cool to eat junk to being cool to be smart eaters. We've let the manipulative giant food companies sneak in 80 chemical additives in my lifetime and destroy the nutrition that used to be in the food that nourished our grandparents very well. We've also had the emergence of 'white food'- white sugar, flour and rice. It is so lacking in nutrients that the body drags nourishment from other areas of the body to digest these.

Cool Teachers can have such an influence by dropping little comments here and there.

"Who had protein for breakfast?"

"What protein foods do you like best?"

"You must have had a good breakfast – you have done really well in your maths this morning!"

"You must be a smart eater."

Testimony About Food Additives

By an adult member of the LD Support group

I'd heard information for years. I'd listened to Barb in discussions we have had from time to time - especially since Barb practices what she preaches on the danger of food additives - but I still drank my Coca Cola & ate my junk food, etc. My attitude was that my body was coping with all I threw at it.

However, I really heard the message one night when I was attending our *Move to Learn* Support Group. It wasn't just Barbara that night talking about the dangers of processed foods but several others as well. This created the decision at last to do something for my brain and body.

Over a couple of months, I listened to others on how behaviour improved, sometimes dramatically, when Tiny Tim or cute Kim had particular coloured cordials, MSG, and 282 removed from their diet. Listening to these adults and teenagers struck a chord in my grey matter and I decided to have a look at some websites. These investigations both frightened me and disgusted me. Multinational companies making big dollars and not caring about family chaos. Well, no more for this bunny.

I started shopping at the 'health shop' area of supermarkets. If you look around, there are actually outdoor markets and stores to accommodate safe eating foods. Yes it's a bit more expensive but guess what – I use whatever I buy. My wasted food at home and junk food buying has cut back dramatically, so I reckon I'm about even in my spending.

I keep hearing about beans being great for protein and I used to mentally deride the speaker with my "if you 'wanna' do it, you go right ahead, me, I'm 'gonna' eat meat cause that's what Aussies do."

Oh my, the power of information! Beans cooked with the right flavours are yummy. Vegetable compote & brown rice, beautiful! Fruit salad instead of toast. Porridge was always a favourite, and for those who don't like it, cook in a few sultanas, finely sliced apple and serve with honey & milk, mmmm. Once I got my brain out of meat, my imagination kicked in & it's good fun. Potato & leek soup is another one, simple and scrumptious. Told you, I'm on a roll. Soy bean sausages, uh uh, don't knock them till you've tried them.

Results of all this effort – easy.

I have spent most of my life being a very angry person. Extremely oversensitive to the slightest criticism and highly defensive. I used to love being angry because it gave me a strong sense of power. I have destroyed relationships, lost friends, lost the trust of workmates and worst of all, despised myself. That's the sort of power I used to wield. Bizarre, isn't it!

Slowly getting off as many food additives as I could resulted in my anger diminishing. Certainly enough for me to see how sad it all was, certainly enough for me to want to work at being a nicer person and certainly enough for me to want to like me. My memory also improved. To try to quantify how much, I would say by 10-15%. Even more exciting, my concentration has improved and my hypersensitivity to noise is calming a little and allowing me to start to tolerate some noises that have always irritated me. (e.g. tiny tots in a group when I am listening to a speaker, etc.)

My road to self acceptance has a few holes and is a bit 'ouchy' pebbly but the 'beaut' part is that my brain, my liver and I now want to continue this journey and no matter how many times I fall off, I'm happy to get back on.

Caroline Smart (*September 2005*)

PS: I now have read that a certain supposed bread preservative is actually a poisonous chemical sprayed on cutting equipment to stop bread mould and it's used so companies can eliminate the need for a person to clean equipment regularly.

A Story Told by a Parent

Claire's Journey to being well

Claire had been presenting with vomiting migraines, stomach pains when she ate, on and off for two years, cramps in her legs after exercise and exercise induced asthma. She coughed every morning and night and when she was having an asthma episode would cough all day and night and need to be given high doses of cough mixture as well as a steroid based medicine on top of her two different puffers. She was on a preventative puffer as well as one for when symptoms presented. The doctor said they were childhood migraines and that she would probably grow out of them. She suggested that Claire keep her water intake up, checked her tight tummy and discussed the stomach pains, and felt it could be a problem with wind and other things I don't remember. Basically, 'nothing too much to worry about'.

Claire started kindergarten in 2003 and suffered terribly from separation anxiety. Her asthma seemed to get worse as her stress levels increased and so did the migraines and stomach pains. I put the tummy pains down to an excuse to get out of going to school, and she suffered from these for another 12 months. During her time in kindergarten she had two severe asthma episodes with vomiting coughing. After a particularly unhappy experience at the half yearly parent Teacher session in grade one, I knew I needed to get help. The Teacher told me that Claire was often doing what she was told not to do and that she didn't pay attention much of the time, and that she had no idea about mathematics. When I asked her if Claire was good at anything the Teacher responded after about a 20 second silence that, "No, she wasn't". Distressed, I contacted a person I had heard about who turned out to be the saving of Claire - Kirsty, who worked with children with Learning Difficulties.

After testing Claire in various areas of reading and comprehension, Kirsty found that Claire's scores were average. Then she did an auditory processing test on Claire and found that instead of her taking 80 milliseconds to hear and comprehend, Kirsty took 200! This explained why Claire was not following the instructions of the Teacher. She was not processing her instructions fast enough.

I then told Kirsty about the vomiting migraines and stomach pains and asked if these were in some way connected. She informed me that it is not okay for children to get migraines and that we needed to find the cause of the migraines and tummy pains – not wait until she grows out of them. She said she could help Claire with her auditory processing problem but wanted me to see a doctor in a near-by city first to look at the migraines and tummy pains.

So off we go for an hour and a half's drive - with Claire, my mother, father and my toddler in tow. Dr. Dyson was about to become one of the most significant people in Claire's and our lives. We had no idea at that first appointment how dramatically she would change Claire's life.

After talking to Dr. Dyson about Claire, and filling in questionnaires and answering many, many questions, she explained we were going to treat the cause and not the symptoms of Claire's problems. It was going to take dedication, patience and time. We were not going to get a quick fix and I felt very, very overwhelmed and afraid that we would not be able to do this.

While we were in her office she noted the Teacher's comments about Claire's mathematics. She put her through a few quick exercises and asked if we could wait an hour and come back and see her Occupational Therapist as she felt strongly that her right and left brain were not crossing over and that this was the cause of the problem with number work and her reluctance to read.

All I could think of was "Oh my God is this ever going to stop – what else could possibly be wrong with Claire! How on earth are we going to fix this?" Before we left her office we were loaded up with pathology forms and more questionnaires and were told that she felt strongly that Claire had some severe food intolerances and was certain an allergy to dust mites was involved in there as well.

We left her office and saw the receptionist on the way out to pay and she looked at me (God knows what the look on my face was!) and she said "Don't worry, everyone has that look on their face when they walk out of Dr. Dyson's office for the first time, but I promise after the second or third visit it will change to a big smile!" I thought to myself – "I don't think so, lady – you have no idea what just went on in that office!!!"

Well, visit number two and Claire's blood tests are back and it's confirmed that she has intolerances in varying degrees to wheat (bad), dairy (bad), oats, liquorice, meta bi sulphites (bad), peanuts, as well as a severe dust mite allergy.

Claire lived on bread; she loved it. How was I going to get rid of that out of her diet without drama, not to mention cheese and peanut butter? All I could think was that this couldn't have been worse news. Dr. Dyson made it clear that these were the causes of Claire's asthma, tummy pains and most certainly the vomiting migraines. In particular, she felt that the wheat and dairy were significant contributors. I mentioned that Claire was diagnosed as lactose intolerant as a baby, and the paediatrician said she would grow out of it by 12 months and that I should start introducing yoghurt and some cheeses from six months to see how she reacted. Obviously she hadn't grown out of it!!! The doctor asked if she had reacted, and I said that she was always unsettled so I didn't really notice when or if she was worse when she ate it, as she didn't sleep much anyway. This certainly explains a lot about Claire's life as a baby and toddler!!!

So off we went with our list of vitamins and mineral supplements, foods to be eliminated from her diet, exercises from the Occupational Therapist to be done every night and a commitment to go on another hour's drive monthly for testing by an Occupational Therapist where we would be given more exercises to do. These included crawling, rocking back and forth on hands and knees, flip flops (see chapter 5) and exercises to make her more aware of her body and where she was in space. I spent the long trip home trying to figure out how I was going to get her to take fish oil twice a day and swallow tablets. As I paid the receptionist I still had 'the look' on my face and she just smiled and said, "It's going to be okay, I promise".

However, we embraced our new regime with gusto and I went shopping!!! Dr. Dyson warned me to give myself two hours for the first time, as I'd need to read every packet. What an eye opener that was. I learnt all about meta-bi-sulphites (which are preservatives from 220 – 228 which are in all cordials – I mean ALL cordials, many soft drinks, most coloured lollies (candies), most ice-blocks etc.) I came to the conclusion that if it looks like it might glow in the dark, it would have those preservatives in them and she shouldn't be having them. I found out that many packets had contact details on the back to contact a person who could guide you to their products that were free of whatever you needed it to be free of.

Claire, to her credit, also embraced this new eating regime (not so much the taking of the supplements) and life started to change within a fortnight. After the next appointment I went to pay the receptionist and she said, "See, there's that smile I was talking about – things are going well then?"

It's been 12 months of OT, food elimination (and gradual reintroduction of some of the foods), constant blood tests to check her allergen levels, sound therapy, kinesiology and continued chiropractic care, but now Claire is fantastic. She hasn't used her asthma puffer since we started. I have actually thrown it away, and she has had only one migraine and this was at Christmas when she ate the wrong foods. Not one stomach pain, and her nasal passages have widened and her ears have started to clear. The zinc and vitamin C has been great for her dust mite allergy. She has had many of the foods reintroduced in small amounts over a week, but I have kept things like the meta-bi-sulphites off the list as they are bad for all children/people and she doesn't miss them anymore. When she wants treats, we buy the natural brand lollies and soft drinks only. (They even do Christmas candy canes, and they are very yummy.)

She is a different child. She was jumping over waves at the beach 4 months into her program and she called out to her dad "I love being on my special diet – I feel so good". The principal of her school said she couldn't believe the difference that has come over Claire – she is a changed child. She is healthy and happy about going to school.

Her mathematics has gone from 'no idea' to the top end of the class, she is reading at an independent level, taking herself off to the school talent quest try outs, swimming like a champion, enjoying life to the fullest, and so are we.

It was a long journey, but it paid great dividends for Claire and us. I learnt the importance of treating the cause and not just relieving the symptoms. This road is difficult to navigate but with great navigators like Kirsty, Shanagh, Michael, Petra and last but not least our wonderful Dr. Dyson to steer you through the ocean of changes - they have made the journey rewarding and exciting. They all kept me on course and focused and I always felt supported. I owe them so much for giving me back my child – a child I had never really known existed.

Tracey Kirk-Downey

10 McAndrew Cres
Mangerton
Wollongong 2500
Australia
Email gtdowney@austarnet.com.au
Ph 02 42264190

Dr. Marilyn Dyson's Story

My background is mainstream medicine and I have worked in General Practice for more than 20 years. When I was in Medical School, there was very little teaching on nutrition. There was, however, a small amount of teaching about allergic reactions to a few foods. There was no teaching about food intolerances nor about the importance of nutrition in brain function.

After many years of work, my personal experience of the pain and fatigue associated with Lupus lead me to try the nutritional approach. I was persuaded by friends and relatives to try a diet that excluded some foods. These foods were the ones that were commonly involved with food intolerances (or sensitivities). I must admit that I was very skeptical that a diet could significantly influence my health. However, within 10 days there was a dramatic improvement in both my pain and energy levels. Then, with the help of an immunologist, I did further work to discover which other foods were problems for me, and I gained even greater improvements.

I looked further into the research in this area. There was a growing body of research, clinical evidence and anecdotal support for the view that foods and chemicals (both natural and added) could negatively affect health, behaviour and performance. Now open to the idea that diet could influence a variety of disorders including Learning Delays (LD), Attention Deficit (Hyperactivity) Disorder (AD(H)D) and behaviour, I started using the elimination diet of the Allergy Unit at Royal Prince Alfred Hospital with my patients.

In 1993, I joined the practice of Dr. Mary Lou Shiel, a wonderful practitioner and a pioneer of the work in this area. She was treating,

Seeing
Dr. Dyson

with good success, food intolerances in disorders such as asthma, eczema, ear, throat and respiratory infections, gut problems, Irritable Bowel Syndrome, AD(H)D and LD. We found that eliminating intolerant foods, healing the gut and adding specific supplements often avoided the need to do the full elimination diet.

By this time I had realised that diet and gut function are the basis of all biochemical reactions and physiological functions in the body. Food provides the basic building blocks to make the neuro-transmitters in the brain. Thus the types of food eaten and the efficiency of digestion and metabolism of these foods are crucial for good brain function. This is also true for optimal health, energy and functioning.

Since 1996, I operated as a sole practitioner, using a holistic approach to treat AD(H)D, LD, behaviour problems and a range of medical problems. In addition to medical and biochemical treatments, I started using neuro-developmental therapies. Along with other practitioners working with children with learning delays and the associated neuro-developmental problems, I searched for, did trials and implemented therapies to improve neuro-development.

These included music based auditory stimulation therapies, sound therapies, visual perceptual and visual motor programs and treatments, general motor and coordination programs and motor programs to integrate primitive reflexes.

More recently I have incorporated a range of new, research-based treatments that have proved effective for the management of Autism and Asperger's Syndrome (ASD), such as the gluten-free casein-free diet, vitamin B12 injections, heavy metal management and specific gut treatments.

Since April 2005 my approach has been revolutionised by the use of the Pfeiffer protocol for treatment of

- AD(H)D

- behaviour problems

- Autistic Spectrum Disorders (ASD)

- Depression

- Anxiety

- bipolar disorder and

- schizophrenia

This research based protocol examines the basic, inherited, biochemical imbalances that are characteristic of these different disorders. These imbalances can be easily identified by blood, urine and hair analysis, and are just as easily treated by vitamins, minerals, amino acids and essential fatty acids.

So far, my results are similar to the Pfeiffer Institute's excellent outcomes. Their outcomes show that they can successfully take 80% of AD(H)D and depressed patients off their medications by the use of the supplements appropriate to their identified biochemical problems. The remaining 20% can decrease their use of medication. Like the Pfeiffer Institute, I am also finding big improvements in the other conditions that have these imbalances. (See Chapter 9m and http://www.hriptc.org).

The combination of the dietary approach with supplements and healing the gut together with these other specific protocols are producing excellent results, which can then be foundational for further therapies specific to each individual's diagnosis.

I find my practice now extremely satisfying, seeing huge improvements in the health and well-being of children like Claire. I still get a thrill when Teachers ring up to ask what I have done to totally change a problem child into a model child. I love seeing kids who were failing or not achieving to their potential starting to do well at school, and to see their self-esteem and confidence rise. They return happy, and the stresses and strains in families are greatly reduced.

It is also very satisfying to see more and more practitioners adopting these methods of treatment.

Good Authorities on Nutrition

- Volunteer assocations

Tracey is right. Not everyone has the support and the resources that she had. There are, however, associations of volunteers who have found success, as Tracey has found with Claire. One of these is the Hyperactivity Attention Deficit Association (NSW) Inc., Australia. They can guide you in your search. It can take a lot of searching to find groups near where you live but if there are none then maybe you and some friends can start one yourselves. That is how they all got started – people looking for answers.

- Lyons, Michael; *Healing the Hyperactive Brain.* Focused Publishing. 2000.

Discusses EFA, Nutritional supplements, water, a healthy gut, exercise and supporting the child's personality. Many, many research findings quoted and discussed in relation to LD.

- Richardson, Alexandra et al. *British Dyslexia Conference.* 2002.

EFA Supplementation for dyslexia, dyspraxia, ADHD 1998 – 2002

A six month study of 102 dyslexic children in the UK taking Efalex, found reading progress was significantly better in the Efalex group than in placebo group. Those children with high deficiency in fatty acids, visual symptoms when reading or ADHD responded most.

- Meiser, Frances M.Ed; *The Brain Train. How to keep our brain healthy and wise.*

An excellent, well diagramned information booklet to help children understand the importance of drinking water, essential fatty acids, protein and movement.

There is plenty of research directed at identifying and eliminating allergy provoking and intolerant foods. Order from www.braintraincenter.org

• Dengate, Sue. *Fed Up – Understanding how food affects your child and what you can do about it.* 1998 Random House.

An excellent easy to purchase Australian book with accompanying web site with recipes and latest commercial safe foods, questions and answers.

• Hawke, Maureen. *Learning Connections. Nutritional and Environmental Factors and how they impact on Learning, Behaviour and Development.*

Valuable information about our toxic environment, pre-conceptual care, ear infections and the importance of their good bacteria, and results of their study on *Child Patterns of Behaviour.* www.learningconnections.com.au.

• Eady, Julie. *Additive Alert. Your Guide to Safer Shopping.*

The essential information about what's *really* in the food you eat, which additives to avoid and why. Her up-to-date 'additives to avoid' list should go on all trips to the supermarket. www.additivealert.com.au

Chapter 5

Getting it into Schools

Chapter 5

Getting it into Schools

Why do we need to implement the program?

In Australia, for the past decade or so, movement programs which address immaturities in the foundational layers of a child's development have been creeping into schools very tentatively. How? One classroom at a time – slowly but surely. I'm not referring to the old gross motor programs that were popular a few decades ago. They were good for most children but those with LD often found them unhelpful. The LD students realized that they were not as good as the other children and spent regular

Avoiding sports

time hiding in the toilets or arranging for 'sick notes' from their parents so they wouldn't have to participate.

Learning Difficulties are often caused by a neurological problem, not an educational one. The conduction of messages, to, from, and within the brain of a child experiencing difficulties with learning, is usually found to be inefficient. As part of this neurological problem, the child may also have primitive reflexes left over from babyhood which prevent freedom of movement and hinder development, and always, in my experience, the two sides of these children's brains, and therefore their bodies, don't work efficiently together. As a result, many of those who struggle academically are not really ready for school when they start and find it hard to keep up with the children who are ready. An eight year old, for example, with the eye movement ability of a four year old, will experience great difficulty competing against a classroom of other eight year olds, most of them able to move their eyes easily without moving their whole head when they read.

Only the eyes should move

It is possible, however, to help these children with retained primitive reflexes, and any unfinished integration of the brain. The *Move to Learn* program has been specifically developed to address these immaturities. It has been shown to be effective, and can be easily incorporated into any school curriculum to ensure that all students in need receive help.

Why is this Program Effective?

• It mimics normal human development.

• It provides stimulation to the body senses.

• It matures the body helping to further integrate the most commonly retained primitive reflexes naturally, through the movement sequences themselves.

What does the Program Involve?

All that is needed is some floor space and a DVD/video machine. Very little preparation is required – except maybe to roll out a plastic mat and turn on the film. The more floor space the better but it is quite possible to use only a classroom with the tables moved aside or going up and down the aisles.

In a very small space, the 'buddy system' works well. Students can be paired off so they can help each other. One does the movement and the other one watches, encourages and answers questions "Is my leg straight?" "Am I doing it slowly enough?". Even if all a child does is watch, he or she will learn by doing that. Then turn about. This is helpful if space and other helpers are short, and is often preferred by the students. They can group around a struggler, sometimes all wanting to help, and the input of a peer can often be less intimidating than that of a Teacher. The Teacher can then put his or her focus on monitoring the children's progress and keeping them on task, which we have found is not usually a problem because they are so anxious to move on as a group to the next challenge.

Teachers are usually advised merely to observe and encourage rather than correct. The children learn by watching the video examples and each other. Even if the child they are watching is performing the movement incorrectly they are still learning. The next day as they watch the exercise on the video something might click. Affirming support from the Teacher/parent when they do them correctly or are trying, is, of course, always helpful and indirect guidance can work well. If the leader notices, for instance, that Mary puts her right arm up instead of down then the leader can comment as the video is played the next day how nicely the little boy on the video is keeping his right arm down. Buddies may be less tactful but they will work it out.

Teacher preparation need not take long. The very best training preparation can occur when the Teachers/leaders first learn to do the movement sequences slowly and well themselves. It can also be a lot of fun getting down on the floor with the children, but if that isn't medically possible, it works well to just use the video and train one or two others to assist in teaching the sequences.

The film itself does the teaching and training about the sequences. It takes the place of someone coming to the school to teach the program.

What is a Retained Primitive Reflex?

All Teachers will undoubtedly have seen students holding their pens so tightly that their knuckles were white.

This tight uncomfortable grip, which makes it impossible to have any kind of speed in note taking, can be the result of a retained primitive reflex.

These are reactive movements, used for survival, which do not require a thinking part in babies' immature brains. They were 'wired in' to help movement in the womb, for birthing and for surviving the shocks of the first few weeks of life. In due course, babies can direct more purposeful movements and they no longer need their original automatic reflexes. In fact, if they are kept they become a barrier to easy natural movement development.

Retained primitive reflexes have long been known to affect learning.

The Lancet, 2000; 355:53-41 refueled interest and work in this area by publishing research on the effects on learning in school children who received intervention which integrated retained motor reflexes.

It is important to be aware of the effect of keeping primitive reflexes beyond their usefulness because it affects both academic learning and social interaction. Symptoms of retained reflexes may also include restlessness in class or at assembly time, immature posture, over-reactiveness and sometimes clumsiness.

Preschool play activity plays an important role in the maturation of these primitive reflexes, but for some children this natural pre-academic phase of learning and development is not completed before the child starts school and the child is therefore unprepared to learn. Sometimes this is simply due to lack of opportunity. Outdoor adventurous play is not always available to children these days but some children will also take longer to mature and will need even more exposure to play activities and to directed movement experiences. They can often be immature and slow at developing confident movement and sometimes as a result people want to overprotect them. These students are usually aware that they are not as good at sports and games as the other children and may back off from participating in the very thing that would make life better for them. It is essential that parents and Teachers give them only activities at which they can achieve and not be embarrassed. The groundwork needs to be laid first.

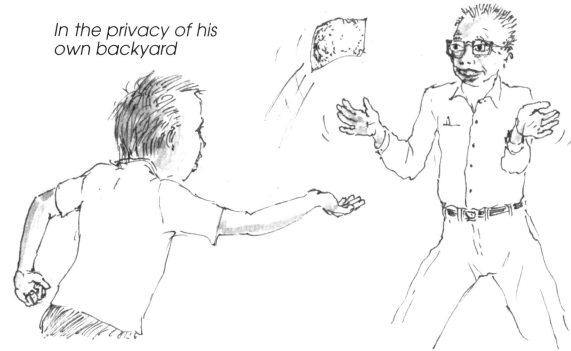

In the privacy of his own backyard

The ongoing presence of primitive reflexes at school age indicates that the lower part of the brain has not reached full maturity. This child then has 'not got it all together'. He may not have good posture or effective control of his body to adequately sense, explore and judge where he is, what is going on around him and what he is doing. The lower part of his brain is likely not automatically picking up and sending good information to the higher thinking, judging, talking, understanding and remembering parts of his brain.

Learning will be affected to some degree in this case. The most common primitive reflexes that are kept by students with Learning Difficulties are described below.

If the Reflexes are kept beyond their usefulness you may see the following Symptoms.

The Symmetrical Tonic Reflex – In hands and knees position, with head looking up, the arms straighten and the hips and legs flex and vice versa. This means that when told to "Sit up while writing!" the arms extend and lose their writing position and eyes focus in the distance. When looking down, the head can get too close to the desk as the arms flex. Crawling with feet off the floor indicates that this reflex may not be well integrated.

Asymmetrical Tonic Neck Reflex – The primitive reflex that can later, if retained, make for this fight with the pen is the Asymmetrical Tonic Neck Reflex (ATNR). When the baby turns his head, the arm towards which the head is turned 'shoots out' and the other arm bends. This makes for a good trip down the birth canal but by six months of age the baby doesn't need it for survival anymore.

*Holding his pen
for dear life*

Some children, however, keep this reflex even into primary and high school even though it is not very obvious. When their heads turn to look at their pens their arms still feel as if they want to shoot out so they tightly grip their pens. This interferes with a more evolved human ability of the top/higher/cortical brain which is able to separate the tripod fingers from the fourth and fifth fingers.

Galant Reflex – The ticklish, restless child, with discomfort around his waist who is constantly hitching up his pants. This can result in poor concentration, poor short term memory, extended bedwetting and a hip rotation to one side while walking.

Constantly hitching up his pants

Palmar Reflex – a clenching response when the pencil touches the palm interfering with a refined finger grip. There can also be tongue movements when concentrating on hand activities.

*An immature
hand grip*

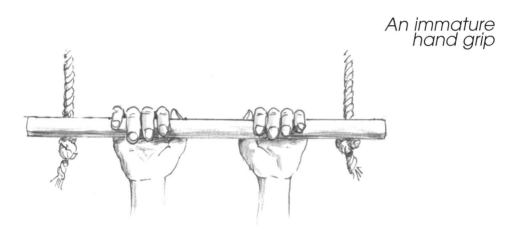

Tonic Labyrinthine Reflexes – difficulty holding the head and body up against gravity causing a posture that finds it almost impossible to sit upright and still in the chair.

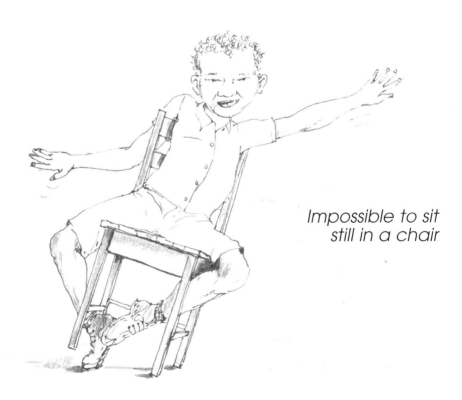

*Impossible to sit
still in a chair*

Neck Righting and Body Righting Reflexes - the body still follows the turning head and vice versa. Body rolls 'like a log'.

Running into a garbage bin

Moro Reflex – over-reactiveness to stimulation – sight, sounds, movement and being bumped and touched – the whole body is 'on alert' causing over-watchfulness, tentativeness, withdrawal or 'the best form of survival is attack'.

Whole body is 'On Alert'

Introducing the Program to the School

An effective way to introduce this program to schools or a group of parents is to show the 55 minute film, *Move to Learn*, over two sessions. The first half of the film will give everyone a more accurate picture of the nature of these difficulties with learning. It shows interviews with members of the main helping professions, apart from Teachers, who often play a vital role in preparing these children for learning.

After watching the video, the group can then discuss what professional help and resources are needed for their children and can formulate a list of what is available in their community.

Implementing the Program

The second half of the film goes through the warm-up exercises and the nine sequences, one at a time. Teachers are shown working with various children and an easily followed commentary explains the correct procedure. This part of the film is designed to be used as a teaching resource. It can be played for the students as a daily prompt for the exercise to be done that day.

Warm Ups

It's best to start each session with the warm up exercises as illustrated on the film. These can also be done as a refreshing break at any other time as well.

1. Breathing – These are general breathing exercises that help to relax and focus the children. Effective breathing relaxes the body and provides oxygen to the brain for thinking.

2. Eye exercises – Eye movement is controlled by muscles which, like all muscles, require appropriate exercise for efficient control. Toning up the 12 extra-ocular eye muscles assists both eyes working together for reading and writing.

3. Monkey Bars – These exercises will help to build up upper body strength to develop a stable base for head and eye control, eye-hand coordination for handwriting. This activity works the body against gravity. It assists in integrating the Palmar Grasp, the Asymmetrical Tonic Neck Reflex and Tonic Labyrinthine Reflexes.

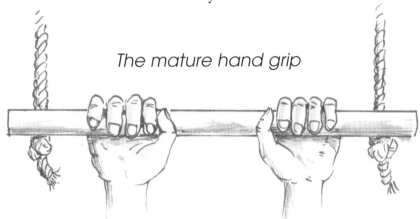

The mature hand grip

The Sequenced Movements

The class should work on these exercises **one at a time**, progressing on to the next movement sequence at the students' pace. Some movements may take longer than others. e.g. Rolling might take several weeks before being mastered, while rocking can be done in less time.

After warm up, the children can progress to the sequenced movements.

For these, it's best to remove socks and shoes – this will allow important stimulation to the body through the soles of the feet.

The whole class should then watch the movement for the day on the DVD/video. If there is no player available the Teacher can demonstrate the movement or have someone else demonstrate it for the children. The important thing is that the class watches it done properly.

The group can then break into pairs to work on it.

There is then usually enough time for everyone to have a 'go' at the current movement. It is good brain stimulation also to go quickly back to a previously learned sequence or forward to a new one as a challenge, if there is time.

1. Rolling

These exercises can be done with arms up and/or by the side to prepare the body for rotating or twisting, an important part in developing balance reactions, enabling the body to learn to allow the head to move independently of the body. (e.g. not riding your bike into the rubbish bin when you turn your head.). They help to mature retained Asymmetrical Tonic Neck Reflexes, (Part of this develops as the hand helps the body shift positions from prone to pushing off), Neck Righting and Body Righting Reflexes and Tonic Labyrinthine Reflexes.

Nausea when rolling is due to an immature vestibular system. If this occurs it is because the eyes and movement sensors in the inner ear and the body are out-of sync and telling the person via their survival system that it's not safe. 'Stop, you can not cope with this!' If this occurs, it will be necessary to stop the full body rolls and substitute side to side head movements instead. These can gently provide the student with small doses of the uncomfortable movement until the vestibular system and associated parts of the brain and body are able to cope better.

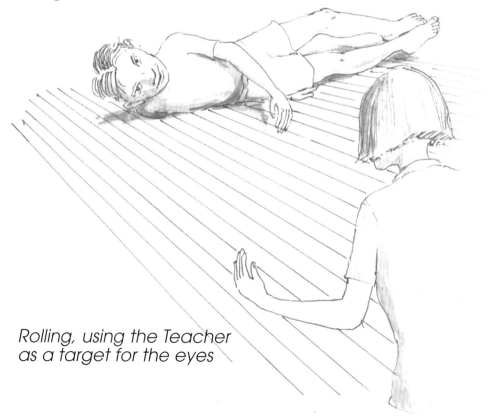

Rolling, using the Teacher as a target for the eyes

2. Gliding on the Stomach

These exercises build up back strength to assist with good posture, and will give the body more opportunity to over-ride the Tonic Labyrinthine Reflex if still retained. Working against gravity in this way is part of the enabling process for babies to develop strength to sit up and for crawling on hands and knees.

OR

Gliding

3.and 4. Unilateral and Cross Pattern Flip Flops

These exercises give the opportunity to further integrate the Asymmetrical Tonic Neck Reflex if still present, and further works on communication between the two sides of the body, to enable sequencing of movements - a vital part of nearly all coordination activities of the hands and legs. Preparation for mathematics.

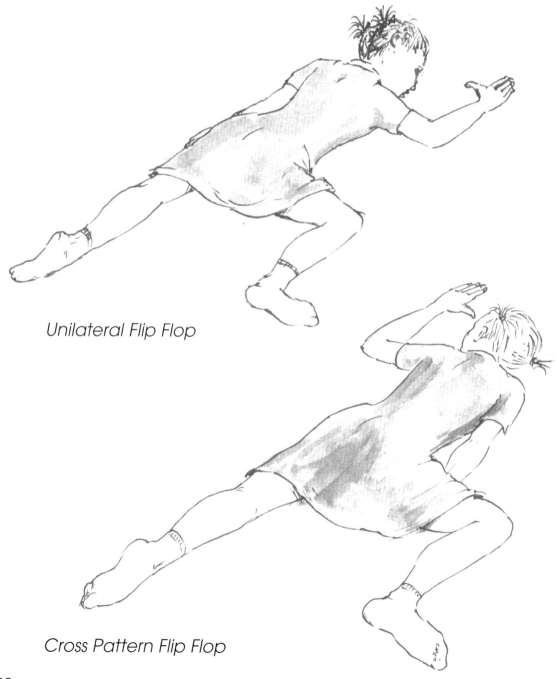

Unilateral Flip Flop

Cross Pattern Flip Flop

5. Stomach Crawling

These exercises further strengthen the neck and shoulders in preparation for eye-hand work and takes the next step in integrating the Asymmetrical Tonic Neck and Tonic Labyrinthine Reflexes and getting both sides of the body to work together and prepare for crawling.

Stomach Crawling

6. Rocking

These exercises are part of the preparation for crawling. They further strengthen the muscles and integrate the reflexes. Flat palms and fingers pointing forward are important to diminish a sensitive retained Palmar Reflex. Circular rocking will exercise the palms of hands to develop palmar arches.(See Glossary)

Rocking back up and down to the count of a Slow Waltz

Optional Excercise – Circular Rocking

7. Unilateral Crawling

These exercises encourage the arms and legs of each side of the body to work together - an important stage in developing laterality and L and R brain/body integrating and further strengthen neck, back, shoulder, arm and hand muscles and help integrate the Palmar Reflex.

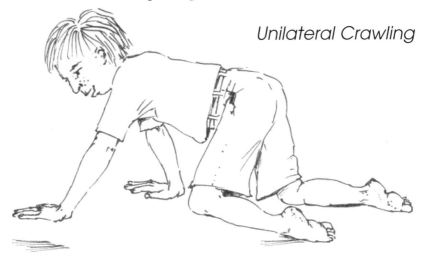

Unilateral Crawling

8. Cross Pattern Crawling

These exercises develop the above to a more mature and demanding level of L and R integration: so much brain work involves information swapping and checking between L and R hemispheres of the brain. Many children with LD have missed this stage in their development and are inefficient in L/R brain processing.

Cross Pattern Crawling

9. Cross Pattern Walking

These exercises enable multi-sensory L/R brain processing.

How long should this take?

The Teacher/leader will know how much time to spend on each sequence because progress is made at the students' own pace. Enough time should be spent on each movement to enable most of the class to do it well, accurately, automatically and slowly. This might take a few days or weeks, and it can take one, two, three, four, five or six months to complete the nine sequences, but it will only take 10 to 20 minutes each day to work on them, and the children won't need to do any more floor work.(The more that is done however, the faster the brain will be stimulated. Anything involving movement will stimulate the brain and promote learning, if the children are having fun).

Cross Pattern Walking

Those students who are struggling with reproducing the movements accurately and easily in class can be encouraged to do it for homework if parents are able to help. It might be a good idea for them to get their own DVD. If they are still struggling, this is a good indication that they might need professional help from one of the fields covered in the first half of the video.

These exercises have proved to be very helpful in pointing to deeper underlying problems that the students may have.

A way of Checking if a Movement has Become Automatic

Once the majority of a class has accomplished the ability to do a sequence in a controlled slow way a Teacher can challenge the class with additional things to do while they are doing the movements.

They can be challenged to do them:

- Blindfolded

- Backwards

- With varying tempo whilst following the beat of a drum.

- While reciting a verse or the alphabet

- While spelling words backwards

- While counting numbers by twos and then backwards by twos.

The ability to do some of these extra things at the same time as they are doing the required movement will tell the leader that her students' brains have been well trained. These extra activities also hold the interest of those who have learned the movements quickly and may need some additional challenges.

If There is Time for Additional Fun Activities

The sequences are only the necessary beginning for academic readiness.

Additional fun activities can be done on days when more time has been allocated.

We have listed a few suggestions below, drawn up by a group of Teachers at our 2004 seminar here at Manly.

- Blowing whistles

- Blowing ping pong balls

- Clapping rhythms

- Animal walks

- Rolling on spine, arms around legs like a ball

- Lying on backs with bended knees and gliding backwards by 'walking' with the feet. This is particularly helpful for desensitizing the back and the Galant Reflex.

- Rubbing parts of own body and identifying them e.g. left knee, right ear

- Drawing letters on the back of student in front who then guesses what it is

- Hugging yourself as hard as you can

- Eye tracking - moving eyes to different places in the room on command

- Tai chi twirls and slaps

- Chewing

- Tracing the figure eight (lying on its side) in the air

- Standing on one leg with eyes closed

- Tapping alternate feet while poking tongue out on opposite side

- Tapping a balloon from student to student, every alternate student etc.

- Playing 'Simon Says'

- Sticking out tongues from side to side can work wonders in waking a group up.

We have found that once one Teacher in a school gives this movement program a go, the results they experience have quickly encouraged other Teachers to join them. It is always helpful to benefit from those who have gone before, worked the details out and can point to results.

There are many Teachers who are successfully using the movement program in their classrooms who have shared with me the excitement they have felt over the success they have experienced. I have listed some of these Teachers and their contact details on my website, www.movetolearn.net, and they are more than happy to be contacted if you have any doubts or confusion about how to implement the program.

Research on the effectiveness of the nine movement sequences is currently being collated by *Move to Learn* through Dr. Christine Chapparo of the University of Sydney. This is described in Chapter 8 and the results will be presented later in 2006.

What Next?

Once the basic movement program has been accomplished, students may want to prepare for participation in a sport with their friends. To this end Veronica Steer has created a helpful outline of what skills need to be taught for several common sports activities in Chapter 9e.

The Nine Sequenced Movements in Summary

Class Teachers as well as leaders of LD Support Groups have found it is helpful to have the pictures of the nine movements put on cards and placed near where their learners are practicing. It enables each person to refer to the appropriate card if desired, so please feel free to copy them if you wish. A3 sized cards can be purchased from *Move to Learn* with the nine movements pictured on them. These can be used for classrooms, practices and anywhere the movements are being done.

Chapter 6

The New Pioneers

Chapter 6

The New Pioneers

6a. From Getting to the Roots of Her Son's Problem to Those of Many Preschoolers

By Winsome Richards, an Education Assistant at Kalgoorlie, Western Australia, and now of Perth.

With a fierce determination to help her son, Winsome accomplished her aim and then turned the lives of many early education, pre-primary children around with her huge bank of experience. She couldn't stop herself from the addiction of wanting to learn more from many courses and sources including ANSUA *(now* Learning Connections) *and* Move to Learn, *and has obtained an Associate Diploma in Social Science Child Care 0 – 5, Central Metropolitan College of Tafe, Perth, WA.* – Barbara Pheloung

My child was born in 1969. I held him in my arms and all I wanted was to be able to love and nurture him and watch him grow into the fine man that he is today.

My son was a bright boy who had a great memory as a little chap, and it was obvious that 'he would do well'. He worked at an above average level until the end of Year 2 and then, inexplicably, by the end of Year 3 his reports started to change. By Year 4 he was below average. How could that be? His spelling and reading in particular had deteriorated.

Finally in 1979 my son's (and my own) frustration levels were rising. I found a private elocution Teacher but fairly quickly she informed me that he was poorly coordinated. At that stage I didn't even know what coordination was, let alone that it could be the reason he was having difficulty with his reading and spelling.

Our next step was to begin a trampolining and motor program, based on a colleague's success with High School students (who had had problems with reading and spelling). Our doctor also referred us to a neurologist in Perth for an assessment and a CAT scan. The neurologist related our son's problem to the vacuum extraction that he had experienced during birth.

Next came an assessment by a guidance officer at the school, and the results were confusing, as they suggested that he had slightly above average IQ, and that 'poor teaching', not 'brain damage' was the cause of our son's problems.

When I next saw the doctor he asked what the Guidance Officer had said; after I told him he replied "What! Well he's your child. What are you going to do about it?" **I look back now and realise that as a parent I had not really accepted ownership of my child's problem and was allowing others to make decisions for me; I was expecting them to solve my child's problem. After all, weren't they the experts?**

My son's schoolwork and self-esteem continued to plummet and his level of frustration increased. One night, during Year 7 he was trying to do his homework, and was becoming more and more frustrated; he sat on the floor beside his bed and said **"Why am I dumb?"**

I replied "You are not dumb. You just have a problem and I am going to find out what I have to do to fix it." **It was then I realised that I**

had to make the decisions and I had to wear the consequences of any decisions I made, be they right or wrong, and if wrong, I had to continue until I found the answer.

We then went to a Naturopath to check out diet, and an Optician to determine eye dominance. The Naturopath told me that the dark brown colour in my child's eyes were the toxins in his system. After eighteen months of changing to a diet based on 1/3 acid, 2/3 alkaline, my child's eyes were light brown and we had not had to make any more visits to the doctor.

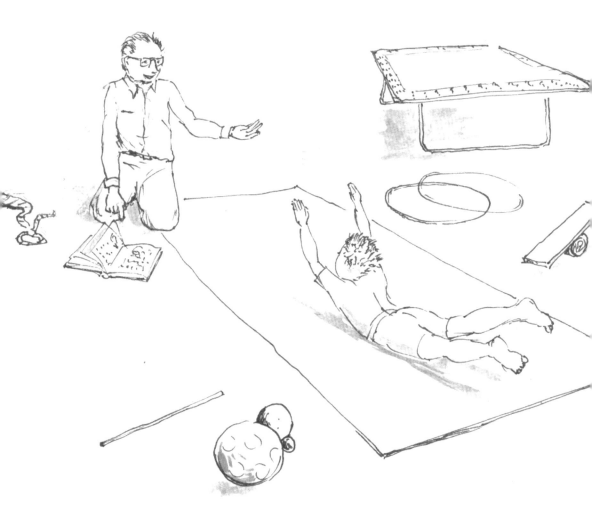

Parents – The managers of their own child's LD

A full assessment with a new Teacher revealed that my son had to concentrate so hard when writing that his pressure on the pencil went through 5 sheets of paper. His eye dominance showed that he was right-eyed for distance, but he alternated eyes when reading and writing.

At this stage my son's classroom Teacher informed me that although Phillip was 18 months behind in his schoolwork, he was actually average for the class.

We started a program with trampoline sequencing, which sorts out comprehension and memory.

We started the program with 100 homolateral flip-flop movements a day and gradually built up to 600. Once he was proficient at this he followed with the same number of cross lateral flip flops, tummy crawls, creeping on hands and knees, and pointing to the opposite foot when walking. This went over a 15 month period combined with eye exercises and a monkey bar exercise (thumbs under the bar). He also attended a Chiropractor and had a small amount of tutoring.

In Year 8 our son was put into a remedial class for English. My husband and I were called in to speak to the Guidance Officer at the High School. She told us that our son had an emotional problem. She thought it best to see him regularly, at his discretion. We agreed. I informed her about the movement program we were doing. She felt that it was probably a waste of time and could be causing unnecessary stress.

He refused to see the Counsellor after a short period of time.

By the end of Year 8 our boy was at the top of the basic class for English and Maths. In Year 9 he went to the top of intermediate English and Elementary Maths. In Year 10 he finished the year with an advance pass in English and was top of his Maths class. This was 'the proof of the pudding'.

He left school, became a chef, travelled the world for 11 months and came back to Australia and went into hotel management training. He now manages a 224 room, 3.5 star city hotel.

Learning & Education

In August 1981, I commenced work as an Education Assistant in Pre-Primary at the local school. Here I began to see many other children whom I felt would have similar problems to my son.

During that year I managed to work in two remedial classes. In these classes the Teachers would explain the program to me and I would implement it with individual children or in small groups. Throughout that time I saw the confusion and frustrations of some of these children, who appeared to have average intelligence yet could only achieve very basic standards of literacy.

In the '90s, I was awarded an Associate Diploma in Social Science and did ANSUA's *Developmental School Program* with Maureen Hawke. This later training reinforced the need to prioritise treatments – the most basic ones first.

I also worked occasionally with *Gymbaroo* in Kalgoorlie. Margaret Sasse started *Gymbaroo* in Melbourne in 1982 and had a marvellous program to help develop children. I highly recommend her book *If Only We'd Known,* as well as her videos on the *"Importance of Being..."* (*Infant; One; Two; Three; Four*). They should be compulsory reading in all universities and T.A.F.E. Colleges where courses are taught on Early Childhood.

In 1997 we contacted Barbara to come to Kalgoorlie. In Kalgoorlie she presented two sessions, to 90 professionals and 60 parents. As a result of this Mrs Margaret Greville began the one semester *Movement/Commonwealth Literacy Program* for a selected group of Year 8 students at Eastern Goldfields High School. For two years in a row Margaret was nominated for a *"Teaching in Excellence"* Award.

A study in 1997 indicated that 33% of children K to 3 at a Junior Primary School in the Kalgoorlie District were at risk. After a *Fundamental Movement Skills Program* was implemented and completed, the follow up testing showed the 'at risk' group to be reduced to 12.3%! (See Margaret Greville's story next)

Testing was carried out in other schools with similar results. Unfortunately, fundamental movement skills in our primary schools still do not cover the basic foundation stages of movement that are so important for academic readiness.

Many Teachers seem to look at intellectual ability and do not consider physical skills to be a contributing factor to a child's ability or inability to master reading, writing and spelling. Until the Education Department recognises the work of people such as Judy Bullus and Peter Coles, Barbara Pheloung, Jill Taylor (King) and the many others who see the whole spectrum of Learning Difficulties as basically neurological, then many of the behaviour and learning problems of students will not be resolved.

6b Commonwealth Literacy Program

By Margaret Greville, a High School Teacher from Kalgoorlie, Western Australia.

Margaret has led the way by introducing developmental movement programs for 14 and 15 year old high school students within the public school system. She is a fearless pioneer, getting down on the floor with teenagers and all of them loving it. She tells her story with considerable humour. – Barbara Pheloung

The Commonwealth Literacy Program (CLP) began at Eastern Goldfields Senior High School, Kalgoorlie, Western Australia in 1998. The first class commenced in July and ran for approximately six months. It was so successful that we have since run five classes - over one hundred Year 8 students have now been through the program.

A number of factors contributed to the birth of the CLP Program. I have been a Teacher of English (and numerous other subjects) in High Schools for thirty three years. Whilst I enjoyed what I taught, I always felt that I had made very little progress with some students - no matter what I did and how much enthusiasm I applied, they didn't learn. They still had poor reading, comprehension, writing, and spelling skills.

In 1997 I worked as the Reading Resource Teacher at the school. My job was to improve the literacy levels of our students. I was not trained as a reading Teacher, other than through the knowledge I had picked up over the years. I worked both in the classroom, supporting Teachers, and with students in small groups. One of my students was a boy named Phillip. He was 14 years old and had the reading age of an 8 year old. Phillip was always in trouble with his Teachers - he lost his temper, played truant, came late for classes, swore at the Teachers, and never completed work in class or at home - basically he was a failure.

I have never met a student who did not want to learn. There have been many students who played up in class; they annoy everyone so much by diverting attention away from their real problem - low literacy

What were we going to do with the money

skills - that they spend much of their time outside the classroom. The Teacher could get on with her job of teaching the other students who wanted to learn, while the miscreant was outside or in an office where he obviously wanted to be, and everyone seemed happy. But when I talked to these students on a one-to-one level they were often defensive, polite, unhappy teenagers. The real problem was not that they had failed to learn - the system had failed to teach them. I knew that another method was needed but I didn't know what it was, and neither, it seemed, did anyone else.

At the beginning of 1998 three things happened that gave me the chance to try something different. One of the Deputies at the school had applied for a Commonwealth Government grant of money (about $26 000) to address the literacy problem at the school. This money was allocated to us in February 1998. No one knew what we would actually do with the money. We had a few hurried meetings, with too many people who couldn't agree on anything. The same old ideas were tossed around – tests, extra help in the classroom, groups of kids being given extra help, etc. But I had tried all that before and achieved little. We needed a new approach.

I had booked to attend a Literacy Conference in Perth. One of the speakers was a reading Teacher from NSW who described how he taught his students using computers - a new concept that I thought would definitely get the kids' attention. The students learnt to read by reading the instructions on computer games, and learnt to write by keeping a diary of their progress and how they felt about their learning. The Teacher was in touch with the students through the diary. I returned to Kalgoorlie keen to use this new method.

Barbara Pheloung arrived in Kalgoorlie at this time. An enthusiastic worker from District Office talked me into attending her Professional Development session, and I felt like a day off anyway. The first thing I noticed when I entered the room, apart from a lot of talkative Teachers, was a board at the front of the room with a long list of problem student labels. I mentally prepared myself for a tiring day wading through how to identify every problem and how we could fix each one. Barbara Pheloung was introduced and I knew that she would have lots of solutions because she was middle-aged and therefore must have some experience in teaching. The first thing that she did was to wave her right arm at the problem list and tell us that they were just lots of different labels for the same problem. At this point I decided that the day was going to be a waste of time – of course the problems weren't all the same. Half an hour later I had changed my mind and was really interested in what she was saying.

After morning tea we were ushered into another room and volunteers were asked for, to do some exercises on the floor. Eventually I stepped forward, because I was one of the few Teachers wearing slacks and also because I felt sorry for the visiting speaker (as no one else was moving). I knew that I would be able to do the exercises because I was educated, I had a university degree and I wasn't a kid with a learning problem.

Ten minutes later I knew that I was wrong again. There were some exercises I couldn't do and I ended up laughing at my embarrassment and frustration. I still remember how I felt, so when I run a movement program I always do the exercises at some stage, with the kids, down on the floor, still getting confused until I clear my mind and really focus on what I have to do. I strongly recommend this for anyone running a movement program. In fact I never ask a kid to do anything that I wouldn't do. I tell them this and occasionally they challenge me. With teenage boys' groups I always run a push-up competition for extra interest and they think it is great because I sag hopelessly in the middle.

After the PD session Dianne Rodgers, from District Office, and Win Richards, a Teachers' assistant from South Kalgoorlie Pre-Primary School, sat with me and we began planning how we would implement a movement program at Eastern Goldfields Senior High School.

It was three months before the first class started - the beginning of Term 3. I had asked Teachers to give me the names of any Year 8 students whom they felt were under achieving, were not chronic truants, and didn't have nasty behaviour problems. (Some kids are so badly damaged that they can't be changed within our system.). From 40 names (out of a cohort of 300) I selected 20 students for the first CLP class. The students met for eight hours each week, during their timetabled English and Math periods. I attended every lesson together with a 'second year out' English Teacher (for four of the lessons) and an experienced Maths Teacher for the other four sessions. Everything took place in one large classroom, which for much of the time must have looked like chaotic bedlam.

Five CLP classes have run at the school, each class lasting for twenty weeks. We now use a separate classroom for the movement program as the kids get quite noisy at times. The original program changes a little with every group, but basically it follows the same format:

• 21 Year 8 students who have learning problems, where their Teachers believe that they are underachieving and they are not chronic truants.

• two Teachers attend every lesson.

• Program runs for 20 weeks.

- All students have their sight and hearing tested by the school nurse at the beginning of the program.

- The group is divided into three teams of seven students each. The group can have boys and girls in it. Each team must be same sexed. (Teenage girls will not roll around on the floor if boys can see them.)

- The program is divided into three parts – movement, computer skills and games, and class work consisting of 'catch up' – primary level work and parts of the normal Year 8 Maths and English Program.

- Each one hour lesson is divided into two parts, and the students rotate through the three activities every one and a half lessons.

A Few Comments

Deciding exactly what to say about CLP classes is difficult. First, they work. The kids love being in them and so do their parents and Teachers. We survey the kids, parents and Teachers at the end of the 20 weeks. Everyone reports changes – calmer behaviour at home and in class, neater hand writing, people can actually read their work, nicer to live with at home, sleeps through the night, volunteers to put out the rubbish bin, doesn't fight with his brothers and sisters, school results have improved, doing better at sport on the weekend, and so the list goes on. When we ran the first class I didn't tell Teachers what we were doing in case it all failed and I had wasted a lot of school money, but I was constantly being asked by other Teachers, "What have you done to that kid? He's changed!" (Comments like that certainly made up for all the broken nights worrying about what we were doing.)

Some students improved during the program, others showed improvement during the following semester but everyone did improve their school results in the months following the course.

We took in an academically weaker identical twin who matched her sister's results within twelve months and passed her within two years. We included a triplet boy who went on to do an apprenticeship, whilst one of the triplets dropped out of school altogether in year ten and the third boy went to work after Year 10.

A number of our Year 8 CLP students graduated from an academic Year 12 course last year – students who in Year 8 would have been expected to leave at the end of Year 10.

We included a Year 8 girl called 'Jane' in the first mixed sex class. 'Jane' was pretty much a mess when we met her – always bursting into tears, "no one likes me", "all the kids pick on me." She'd hide outside the room or crawl under the desk and sit on the floor when she was upset – very frustrating to try to teach! Everything was too hard. In Year 9, twelve months after leaving us, she asked me to sponsor her in a book reading marathon (she'd never read books before!). Whilst she was in Year 10 she told me how she was coping with her older sister who had become heavily involved in drugs, was stealing from the family and had left home. I was amazed at how 'Jane' was coping, was able to see a future for herself and could talk quite rationally to me about it all. I saw her last Thursday with a huge smile on her face, talking to one of her old Teachers on our campus. She is in Year 12 now, and had 'just popped over' to our campus. What a lovely young woman she has become and what a warm spot I have for her.

I took a break from running the classes for a couple of years, as I was starting to feel dull and needed a change, and my husband was very ill. We are starting a new class next week and I'm really looking forward to it. When Teachers start to feel tired of the whole thing it is better to stop for a while, let someone else run it or just call a halt for a semester. You do need lots of enthusiasm and it is exhausting at times, but the results do wonders for your ego.

6c A Teacher's Aide Ends up Teaching Teachers

By Julia Dive, a Teacher's aide located on the south coast of NSW, Australia

Julia's journey is inspiring because most of us felt that we needed our degree before anyone would listen to us, or give us the chance to use the knowledge we had gathered from our experiences with LD children or from books and courses. Let her tell her own pioneering story. – Barbara Pheloung

A friend asked me to work with her 8 year old daughter, who was having trouble keeping up with the rest of the class, and who was becoming upset and depressed. This is how I encountered the world of Learning Difficulties. I soon discovered that the last thing this child needed was more bookwork; there were other issues involved.

I began to research as widely as I could, and was appalled at the lack of availability of books and techniques on the subject. My sister-in-law lent me *Overcoming Learning Difficulties,* and I thought the holistic approach was a good idea. I could visualise some of the children I worked with in the pages of that book, and I was especially taken with the non-academic indicators with which these kids present - because they are the ones we have to live with! However, sitting reading that book on my verandah in a tiny town on the far South coast of New South Wales, Australia, I was overwhelmed by the isolation and lack of professional services in our area. How could I get a look at all aspects of the child when the nearest Paediatrician was three hours away? We had no access to an Occupational Therapist and I had never even heard of a Behavioural Optometrist! I figured that this book *Overcoming Learning Difficulties* may hold a solution for city kids but I couldn't see it happening down here.

I put the book aside and continued my search. As a Teacher's aide I noticed more and more children at peril in the classroom.

A year later Barbara Pheloung came to speak at Eden (only an hour and a half away) and Teachers and Teachers' aides were invited. After spending the day listening to Barbara, and recognising so many traits in the children whom I knew were struggling in the class room, I decided to re-read *Overcoming Learning Difficulties*. I wanted to test out Barbara's techniques on a small group of children. I dismissed the reservations I had about specialist help and decided I would just do what I could, and see if that made any difference - after all I had a verandah and a trampoline! I hoped the rest would follow. A fellow Teachers' aide who was also a mother and friend agreed to help me. So for one and a half hours, three afternoons a week for six weeks, we had six girls ranging from Year 1 to Year 5 come and do activities on my verandah and in the backyard.

We did a reading, spelling and phonemic awareness test, so we could gauge any academic improvement, and then plunged in. It was a fairly intensive 6 weeks but what a lot of fun we had! On mattresses on the verandah we did rocking, rolling, combat crawling, unilateral crawling, cross crawling, unilateral flip flops and cross flip flops. I relocated an old wooden ladder and a long piece of wood (a balance beam) from our shed and I borrowed a punching bag and a mini tramp. Over those 6 weeks, and amongst other activities, we jumped, hopped, swung, skipped, did things backwards, forwards and blindfolded, balanced, sucked, blew, punched, drew with one hand then the other and then both together, drew with our feet, marble painted, played with shaving cream, had a texture bath, drew around ourselves and jumped the trampoline sequences. We challenged all our senses in every way we could and what an insight we gained into those girls.

What surprised me the most was the confidence boost the girls experienced. "I'm not too scared to put my hand up in maths now – even though I'm still not sure of the answer"! Even the couple of children without Learning Difficulties who had joined us, showed improvement in their confidence and general attitude to school. Those in the group whom we knew for sure had academic problems, also experienced problems in the activities and exercises. This backed up everything I'd read in Barbara's books. We discovered the youngest (who really only tagged along because her sisters were there) had Learning Difficulties. Due to this discovery, we were able to ensure early intervention and reduce a lot of the troubles she may have experienced otherwise. She now wears Irlen lenses (see Glossary) and though she still has some problems with literacy and numeracy, she is the School Captain this year! By the end of the program all the girls had improved academically! Barbara's methods were so successful that I decided that for Primary school students whom I tutored, I would mainly do movement, with a bit of literacy and numeracy thrown in along the way.

Woven through this process were long conversations with lots of Mums about kids who "always knocked over the water at the dinner table" and "never did really crawl, you know." As I continued researching, I discovered and confirmed the validity of *Sound Therapy, Brain Gym*, the *Irlen Syndrome* approach, and other bits of useful information. I used the questions out of *Overcoming Learning Difficulties* and others. The Mums answered these which indicated the immaturities and where to start the therapy. A few more children began coming to me once a week. There was always improvement and a lot of satisfaction all round.

Two years later I moved house. I was unable to continue tutoring. I didn't have a verandah anymore. I was less accessible. We were about to extend the shed to hold the tractor implements when I realised it was the perfect place for the movement program. The tractor implements are still outside in the weather but better than a verandah - **I have a shed**! We still use the wooden ladder and the long bit of wood, but have bought a punching bag and a mini tramp. We put up a whiteboard and a blackboard and my husband very generously made a scooter board and a rocker board. The trampoline sits just outside.

When parents come to me now – and it is still only by word of mouth – they answer the questions from *Overcoming Learning Difficulties* and a few others, so we know what the child's needs are and where to start. They can then buy the book or get it from the library and locate the sections which most apply to their child. This empowers them, as they have something they can work with at home. The hour a week the child has with me then has a variety of activities focusing on those areas.

LIFTING THE LID OFF YOUR GARAGE!

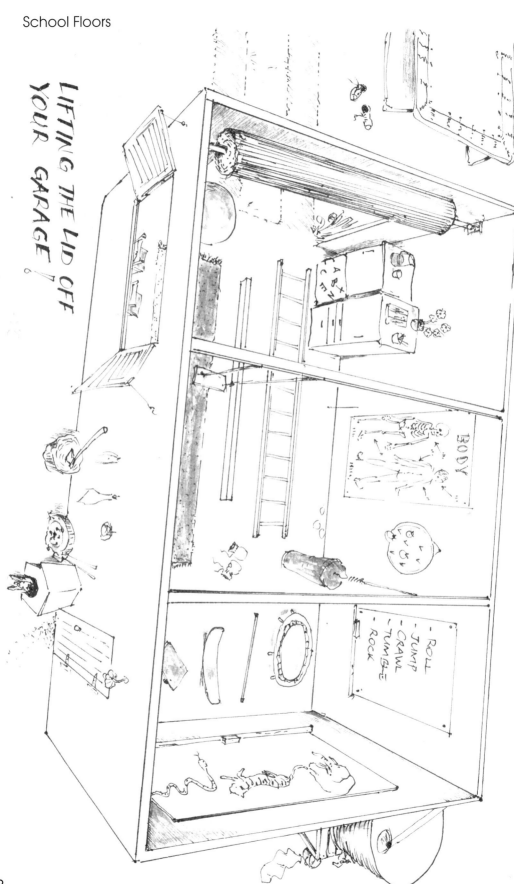

BODY

- ROLL
- JUMP
- CRAWL
- TUMBLE
- ROCK

Some tips I give the parents:

- Maintain a good working relationship with your child's Teacher.

- Have your child's vision checked by a Behavioural Optometrist (we even have one of them now).

- If necessary, have your child checked for Irlen Syndrome.

- Get an objective assessment of your child – Dept. of Community Health has a Speech Therapist and Occupational Therapist.

- Assess the need for *Sound Therapy*.

- Start and maintain a file keeping all records of your child's health and development. Get a report in writing from every professional they visit. (When this child sits the Higher School Certificate he may be able to get special consideration, including extra time or particular conditions, but only with documentation.)

- Find something your child is good at outside of school.

- Realise that academia is such a small part of life. It's just that school takes up a large part of the day.

- Acknowledge it's not easy living with someone with Learning Difficulties. It's a fine balancing act of accepting them for whom they are and helping them reach their potential.

I don't do any academic testing anymore. The kids hate it, 'it's just more school work'. The parents don't really want to know the reading age of their child, they just want a child that will get up and happily go to school in the morning. A child who doesn't come home throwing themselves on the bed in tears because school is such a dreadful place and a child who won't say "Mummy I want to go to sleep and never wake up because I don't get it the way the others do and I'll always feel so dumb and stupid"! The real test is whether they hold their heads higher, how they face the continuing challenges of life and whether they feel more confident about themselves.

The school I work at asked me to run a development day on the work I do in my shed. We went through the steps of neurological development. I demonstrated how it feels to be a child with Learning Difficulties in the classroom. We experienced *Sound Therapy* and an *Irlen Screening*. We got down and did flip flops, crawling and ladder activities.

"I have been a Teacher for over 30 years and am a grandmother and you've told me things today I never knew".

"I've just realised that a boy I had a few years ago wasn't deliberately naughty, he just needed more help".

"We have tools and techniques we can take back to the classroom and implement tomorrow".

As a result of that day we now do regular movement in the infants' classroom. We work our way around the desks, doing mat work, mini tramp, balance beam, tunnel and ladder, all to music. The kids love it and it's a great start to the day. During the day we flip flop the alphabet, sometimes counting or spelling our names. We march and do walking while pointing.

Unbelievably, I was asked to give a presentation at the Sound Therapy Summit in Sydney in 2004 on Children and Learning Difficulties. This was attended by many alternative health practitioners, and was a great chance to give an understanding of the plight of children with Learning Difficulties (and their families) to professionals not involved directly with schools. **There were many useful overlaps discovered with those working in the health field with adults.** It was great to get together with other professionals and find common ground.

Who would have thought that any of this would happen? I don't run a business, I don't advertise, I don't know everything. I just do something with kids - that works.

6d Enhancing Learning Through Movement.

By Sue Mackay, a classroom Teacher at Urunga Public School, Urunga, NSW, Australia

Sue tells how the Move to Learn *program was brought to her public school in a town in rural NSW by the mutual commitment of students, staff and parents. She has inspired the other Teachers in her school as well as all the schools around her, and this is the type of networking we need to accomplish our vision – getting developmental movement into the curriculum of every classroom in the world. It's not going to happen without people like Sue and schools like Urunga. Sue has shared her letter to parents, schedules etc. with us, and they are included in Chapter 9g.* – Barbara Pheloung

At Urunga Public School, our *Move to Learn* Program arose primarily out of frustration – frustration because we had students who were not responding to school initiated programs as we had hoped. The school had instigated a number of sensory programs for students which, whilst most beneficial, needed to be a part of an umbrella approach to learning needs. Students were involved in *Brain Gym*, visualising/verbalising, speech programs, Occupational Therapy assessments and quality educational programs.

Students in Years K-2 had previously participated in a gymnastics program delivered by an external provider. Teachers reported positive changes in student physical skills and enjoyed the concept of daily time slots for physical programs.

It was time however to develop a program of our own, which whilst meeting the physical development skills required of our curriculum, also included the philosophies we had experienced through professional training. A 'learning through movement' program was in the drawing board stages. As an experienced staff, we knew what we required of a program but where did we find it? The answer was to develop it ourselves. As part of the preparation we attended a *Move to Learn* Seminar run by Barbara Pheloung.

Off the Starting Blocks

Teachers on all Kindergarten, Year 1 and Year 2 classes were exposed to this professional learning day. We bought Barbara's resources and pored over the content. With the practical input she had given us and the resource support provided, we knew we were on to something which would meet our needs.

First Steps:

Utilising the philosophy of Barbara's program, we developed a series of activities which could be implemented in the school setting with six classes of young children. The first ten weeks focused on the basic movements including rolling, flip flops and crawling patterns. Five activity stations were developed for each fortnight of the ten week period. Student progress at each station was monitored and determined the activities included in the next round of the program.

The First Year

After two 10 week blocks of the movement program, evaluations were undertaken. Teachers, students and parents were surveyed for their opinions and perceptions. Student data was gathered and compared to the benchmark information collected during the program's initial weeks. Such data included reading levels, behaviour records, visualising/verbalising records and handwriting samples.

Results from our first year of *Move to Learn* include:

- Significant improvements in visualising/verbalising exercises.

- Fine and gross motor skills improvement across Stage 1.

Increased level of participation at Sports Carnival.

- Handwriting improvements - significant in 50% of students.

- Reading levels: Levels to date indicate we can expect increased performance across Stage 1.

• Quality of student writing improved in line with visualising/ verbalising indicators.

• Students report a high level of enjoyment in program. 100% of returns!

• Positive parent involvement as group supervisors.

• Significant improvement in on-task behaviours in class. Settling quickly and finishing tasks.

• Reduced behaviour referrals for Stage 1.

• Increase in the time allocated to fitness/sport activities.

• The big one - all parties are keen to undertake the program again next year.

What Was Next?

The overwhelming results of the first year of implementation gave us the confidence to move forward with our program. For the second year of *Move to Learn* we were conscious of providing physical movement activities for a range of student needs. Kindergarten students, new to school, would undoubtedly benefit from participating in the program developed in the previous year. **They were at very different 'skills levels' and 'needs levels' to students who had successfully completed the first year of the program.**

We were also very conscious of the fact that the philosophy underpinning *Move to Learn* needed to be maintained, even as the physical skills of students had grown. The solution was to develop a further twenty weeks of activities for our continuing students.

The Fundamentals

A significant component of the success of the implementation of a consolidated K-2 *Movement Program* has been to keep things simple. The movement activities programmed needed to require minimal equipment. This was important not only due to equipment costs,

Come rain or shine

but also the implications for setting and packing up time and for equipment storage.

The program is overseen by **a Teacher's Aide**, who co-ordinates the daily program and the skills tracking sheets. This has minimised disruption to class time, freed Teachers, and ensured a commitment to participation four mornings per week. Parent helpers at each station on each day ensure supervision is at a high level. Participation by parents provides them with a valued way to contribute to the school and their children's lives.

Interest from Surrounding Schools

We have had the pleasure of sharing our program with many schools over the last two years. Their interest has arisen because we can honestly say our program works. In its simplicity, schools have been able to see that this would work for them. **No fancy equipment, no huge cost – just a commitment to improve the learning outcomes of students through a multifaceted movement program.**

And….

Teachers talk continually about 'a crowded curriculum'. Time is precious. Interruptions are a weekly occurrence. Stage 1 staff has made a time commitment to *Move to Learn*. School interruptions during the programmed morning timeslots are discouraged. Rain or shine *Move to Learn* goes on. The greatest indicator of the success of the program is the commitment displayed, from the children and by staff. The kids love going and what's more we can see results.

It is working. It is meeting student needs. It is manageable.

Move to Learn at Urunga Public School is here to stay.

6e *Move to Learn* in Michelle Learmouth's Classroom, Sydney, Australia

Michelle is to be congratulated for the way that she has been able to empower parents. She has not only tapped into the wonderful support and strength that parents can offer to a classroom Teacher but she has greatly increased their understanding of what is happening through movement. This means that they can go on learning and helping their child, and hopefully many others, long after her class has moved on. She has also clearly demonstrated that the movement sequences are much more effective the more they are done. – Barbara Pheloung

I was first introduced to Barbara's *Move to Learn* program when I was a child and a relative was attending her Beach House in Manly. Ever since, I have been a big believer in the link between movement and learning because the difference it made to that child was amazing. I studied teaching at university with a Major in Special Education. Early in my career I taught a class with a high proportion of children experiencing various Learning Difficulties. At this school I was reminded of Barbara Pheloung when my principal gave me a copy of Barbara's book, *Help Your Class to Learn.* I used many of the activities in the book for the children on Individual Educational Programs and we saw great progress in fine and gross motor skills and academics.

In my third year of teaching I had a kindergarten class and decided to use the movements in the book more regularly. A few times a week I would go to the hall and the children would perform the exercises. Many of the children were struggling and I felt like I needed to be working with each child individually, as the majority were having difficulty completing the exercises. It became very obvious that the children who had the most difficulty with the movements were also experiencing the most difficulty in the classroom.

Later in my career I found that one of the two students in my class was very good verbally but hated writing. He disliked it so much that he came to the point where he just refused to write. Once again I returned to Barbara's books, and being quite late in the year decided to call her up for some advice. This child was having difficulty with the most fundamental of all movements, rolling. Every morning I would work with him before school and he loved doing all the exercises. As weeks passed other children from my class began to ask if they could join in and the group began to grow. Unfortunately the movement program wasn't backed up at home and we were making slow progress. He did however, become more confident in the classroom and began to apply himself more and disrupt the class less.

At the end of that year I decided to change from classroom teaching to working as a specialist Teacher of children with Learning Difficulties. I began work in a K-12 school doing just that. I attended Barbara's four day workshop and gained many more practical ideas and broader knowledge of the 'how and why' behind the movement program. I implemented the program for 10 minutes a day three to four times a week, with a group of six Kindergarten children and a group of four Year 4 children with whom I was doing remedial work. None of these children were able to complete the activities prior to the program. One of the kindergarten parents borrowed the video from me, and worked on the movements at home on a daily basis with all the children in her family. Her child was at the bottom of my remedial group and over the year made the greatest progress, overtaking most of the other children and impressing his Teacher with his amazing academic progress and increased energy levels. The other children in the group made great gains as well. At the end of the year, two of the children were ready to return to working with the whole class and another one of the parents had decided to borrow the video and continue the program at home. My Year 4 students loved the exercises and we did them in the hallway before beginning our reading lesson. These children would ask to do the exercises every day and were keen to master them. They became more confident throughout the program and were proud of their achievements. Once again not all these students were able to master the whole sequence in the 10 weeks we worked on them.

The following year I decided to return to the classroom. At the beginning of the year I discussed the movement program with all my parents and explained the philosophy behind it. The parents all wanted me to start the program on a whole class basis and a

Parental involvement

couple of the parents requested the video. As a result, one of the students began attending Occupational Therapy and his mother worked on exercises every day before school. There were significant improvements in his academic work and behaviour. At the beginning of the year this student was being pulled up by other staff members for bad behaviour – he was disrupting other students and rarely completing work. Now, six months later he is writing stories on his own, rarely being pulled up by other Teachers and is more settled in the classroom. He has not mastered all the movements in the movement sequence at this stage but has made great gains in his gross motor skills and strength through additional exercises.

Throughout term 2, each week my class was given an activity from the movement program to master for homework. Each student would demonstrate it at the end of the week and we would repeat it or move onto another exercise. At mid-year interviews, parents discussed the difficulties their children had with the movements at home - most of these children were performing at the lower academic level in class. During interviews parents also commented on the improved behaviour and academic progress of their children. A couple of parents requested more information about the movement program. The overall behaviour in the classroom has improved and children's fine motor skills have also improved.

In schools it can be difficult to gain daily access to the hall, and classrooms are limited for space. Some children find it difficult to be sensible under the tables and chairs so I have children spaced around the classroom in groups. There are children doing the exercises on the floor while the others are watching, counting or mimicking while standing up. Then they swap. I have also found that the children don't mind being in a confined space and learn to move without colliding with each other. I am currently involved with Barbara's research on the relationship between movement and learning. As part of the research we were asked to do no movement program for the first month. As we started to incorporate the specific movements I became more and more aware of a noticeable improvement in the children's attention span, willingness to stay on task and work independently.

Over the years, what I have discovered is, to get a recognisable difference the exercises should be completed on a daily basis for 10-15 minutes. When doing this I noticed academic, behavioural and self-esteem improvements with students becoming more confident. I have found that discussing the DVD/video at parent information evenings is a great way to prepare parents to participate, and gives parents who are looking for answers a terrific starting point. Many are keen to watch them at home, and everyone who has borrowed it has thanked me and taken something practical from it.

Having the exercises sent home for homework each week was a great way to speed up the progress of the program; it included the parents and heightened their awareness. The students enjoy watching the DVD and mimicking it, but if you don't have a television in your classroom, then training a couple of students to do demonstrations also works well. **Students are able to identify when someone is doing it incorrectly and will often work with that student to help**

them master it. I have found children take a lot of pride in being able to do these exercises, especially when they feel the changes and see their own improvements.

Carol's
Swimming
Group

6f A Remedial Teacher Converts her School to a Holistic, Movement Based Approach to LD

By Carol Hewatt, resource Teacher at a Private, non-government school in Sydney, Australia.

Carol tells her amazing journey as a reading or remedial Teacher who has come to a place of real understanding of why her students were struggling. We follow her on each stage of her 'eye openers' as she broadens the base of her work and discovers how to use movement most successfully, becoming not only 'a convert' but also 'a spreader of the good news'.
– Barbara Pheloung

If you like detecting and solving puzzles, then helping children with Learning Difficulties might appeal to you. I love it. A parent or Teacher presents me with a child, seemingly not reaching his potential and I try to put the numerous pieces of information together to assess his Learning Difficulties. The big question is always **why** he has difficulties.

The last five years have been an exciting learning curve for me as I have re-entered teaching. Few of my experiences in Teacher training, primary and infants teaching, tutoring, schools in Papua New Guinea or bringing up four children prepared me for the diverse changes in Learning Difficulties in 2000.

Six years ago a friend convinced me to do a *Spalding* course. *Spalding* is a multi-sensory system of teaching phonics. I was a little hesitant, as I thought I had always retained enough phonics in teaching and tutoring reading. I was wrong! This method made sense to me and led to my employment in Sydney, at a boys' school Years 2 – 12, where the whole primary from Years 2 - 6 was taught *Spalding*. My job was to take small groups from each class. These boys needed remedial *Spalding* work. They came with the Teachers' comments of 'lazy', 'doesn't concentrate' and 'should try harder'. I worked hard with them, thinking up innovative ways to enthuse them, motivate them and teach them. During the first year of this I kept wondering what was wrong, as they were intelligent boys, willing to work for me but just not advancing compared to the effort extended. What was wrong?

It wasn't until we started to do Christmas craft that I began to understand some of the underlying problems. It was an eye opener for me! Most of the boys couldn't 'see'! Well, they could see all right but, as I found out later, they had problems with their eyes working together. They had learnt to compensate in numerous ways. "How do you see the board?" I asked one boy.

"I just always go out the front and sharpen my pencils to see what's written", he explained.

Fortunately the school was near to a Behavioural Optometrist, Sue Larter. She is typical of consultants and professionals working with children with Learning Difficulties. They are extremely generous with their time, expertise and knowledge, and look at the whole child, not just their own area. Sue was the first of many to help me.

One of my daughters went to a presentation by a doctor (Marilyn Dyson) who had a child with Learning Difficulties and was working and researching in the area. I started to read all the books Dr. Marilyn Dyson had recommended, and these led on to many others. There were more immature areas than just visual problems in these boys!

By now I was searching for more information. I found a little book, *You Can Read* by Launcelot Johnswood. It wasn't the usual 'how to teach reading' - it proposed to help overcome reading and spelling problems without laborious or costly tutoring. The method was simply a physical exercise program for fifteen minutes a day. The case histories were surprising. Unlikely, I thought. Then Barbara Pheloung's book *Overcoming Learning Difficulties* reinforced the place of movement in development.

I thought it was worth a try. I would try it for a term of 10 weeks. I tentatively explained it to the primary head who encouraged me to try it, despite wondering what I was doing. The initial testing of spelling and reading took two weeks to finalise. Then we started. I had the book in one hand as we followed each exercise explicitly and learnt from each other as we went.

The organisation was minimal. There were two groups of 10 to 15 comprised of the boys already in the remedial classes. The first group missed morning line up and assembly and then about ten minutes of class to make twenty minutes for the exercises. The second group came quickly after recess or lunch so class time missed was minimal. Our only available area was the corridor. Teachers zig zagged over boys doing flip flops, TVs were wheeled around us and we were known as 'Carol's swimming group'. We persevered for ten weeks, 'selling' it as brain challenging exercises. The boys were enthusiastic, though perhaps that was just to miss class (especially the group that missed Spanish) and they always wanted more! With the initial group I did daily eye exercises, flip flops (called homolateral patterning) for two weeks, the slide (not as popular over the carpet) for two weeks, homolateral crawling for two weeks, cross lateral crawling and then the cross lateral walk. I added some Brain Gym for variety. I explained what we were doing, and why, to the Year 6 - and only lost one boy who could not cope with crawling.

Then the extensive retesting showed (a surprise and a relief) all the boys gained 1-3 years in reading and spelling. Unbelievable – I couldn't manage that in small groups or one to one in that time! I knew this as class tests had demonstrated it, and the boys who wanted more had the best improvement!

So this works. I had proved it – but why? I read all Barbara Pheloung's books. I started another group. I added in exercises from her books. I read all I could on primitive reflexes, such as Sally Goddard's book *Reflexes, Learning and Behaviour*. I was able to go to meetings which Sue Larter organized. Knowledge was shared there and I learnt from many speakers and therapists. With more knowledge I now refined the other exercises, keeping the basic five in place.

No one therapy or idea has the whole answer. I found it vital to look at the learning pyramid (*Help Your Class to Learn* by Barbara Pheloung, page 27) and work from the foundation developmental areas and then build on them. The movement program is a part of this and to be most effective should be in the right sequence.

Now I was looking at visual and auditory processing. I trialed a visual testing program *'Vision Screening for Schools'* and have since tested almost all the primary and secondary students, finding nearly 20% with visual processing problems. Visiting and talking to therapists in Neurofeedback and Samonas Sound Therapy has led to many being helped in the neurological development of the child. While people working in these areas over the years have success stories, it is exciting that neurological research is now catching up to show why.

I was privileged to attend Barbara Pheloung's four day Seminar in 2004. This drew together all my reading, put it in order and enthused me to keep going. It is great to network with a growing number of others working in this area. Thank you Barbara and Veronica Steer for your amazing teaching.

At school I have had several Teacher training sessions. I made the mistake of trying to tell them all I know in one session! I have had other consultants talk about their area of expertise. I have demonstrated the exercises to Teachers and to individual classes. I have made a video to show what Year 2 cannot do with ease e.g. march, skip, and balance, and how this correlates with Learning Difficulties. I have spoken to parent functions about it. This has met with mixed reactions of course. I expect scepticism. I was sceptical at first. Teacher training has not included neurological development in the recent past. My daughter has been teaching for five years with no knowledge of how to cope with the growing number of children with Learning Difficulties. Nor is there any difference now. My other beautiful and smart daughter who is at present doing her Teacher training at university finds these ideas vetoed there. Parents, too, need guidance in whom to approach and in what order to help their child. Barbara's book *Help Your Child to Learn* is great for this.

This term I have had two groups again. This is the third year I have done the movement program and there are some changes from my tentative beginning. I now test all Year 2 on entering the school. Tests determine those with primitive reflexes, who are not integrated, have vestibular problems, visual and auditory processing problems and others. These are usually a good indication of some difficulty with ease of learning. These boys do the movement program called the BMX class and then may be sent to a consultant if there is an extensive problem. I add other exercises which work on specific reflexes. The boys roll down the corridor, rock on hands and knees, do postural exercises and have fun. A long piece of lino is popular for commando crawls. Music is used with some exercises.

I add fun ones too and often have boys begging to be in the class. They love bean bags, hoops and especially the large skipping rope doing snakes, waves and mastering skipping. Sometimes we go outside and roll down the hill and do wheelbarrow walks. The large group is no trouble to manage but with one rule - don't touch anyone else. However, individual reflexes may need more work as I have to treat them as a group. I always include breathing exercises and encourage the boys to drink water.

Throughout the term I emphasize that these are brain exercises. When they have mastered the cross lateral crawling I ask them what differences they have noticed. They often say "I read for more than five minutes now".

"Maths is easier."

"I like school now."

"I sleep better."

It is important they can see a difference, and of course confidence and self esteem improve. Some parents watch and will comment on changes, but I have not used parents to help. The Teacher's aide is an expert in noticing correct movements. I do not do extensive pre and post academic testing now. I do use handwriting and 'drawing a man' as well as simple reflex testing to indicate those to include in the group. Teachers are becoming more aware of problems and looking at the 'why' of Learning Difficulties rather than expecting the child under stress to try harder.

I notice that these boys are more likely to be awarded for 'most improved', 'trying hard', 'concentrating well', 'handwriting is easier'. For some this may also mean a 'catch up' remedial program. If everything is now in place developmentally this can be done easily.

A letter is sent home and parents invited to ask for more information or visit the school to watch. I explain the role of primitive reflexes to parents. I discuss briefly how these lead to postural reflexes and when these are in place there is ease with academic subjects.

Last week the primary school voted to use the movement program in each classroom. I am so excited about this as it means all boys will have a chance to change. I have found that even the brightest child may still have primitive reflexes not integrated and while he is able to find ways to compensate for this difficulty, there is still some stress or difficulty in learning. The Teachers will do pre and post tests and a behaviour checklist, and will be diligent in giving the program an opportunity to succeed. One class has already seen changes with a modified program this term. A boy with Down Syndrome, who has been doing the exercises for two years, has now perfected them. This has coincided with an amazing progress in reading, spelling and writing. It is exciting to have such a simple way to make a difference to the growing problem of Learning Difficulties.

6g Mental Diseases and Learning Difficulties are Both Neurologically Based

From Rachel Fisher, trainee Counsellor, NSW, Australia

The way that Rachel is using the movement program has warmed my heart. For years now I have become more and more aware of the need to include the awareness of the neurological nature of Learning Difficulties in the training of Counsellors. I also love what she has said about movement with adults. I have heard very good reports from nursing homes when movement work is done, even in wheelchairs, with the type of movement tailored to each person's capability. – Barbara Pheloung

I am training to be a Counsellor and am excited about the possibilities of this *Move to Learn* program for the people I will see in the counselling room. **There is a large overlap between the Learning Difficulties field and the counselling field.** Counsellors see many clients that have Learning Difficulties. However, if the Counsellor is unaware of the complexities that are unique to Learning Difficulties, they can be hard to separate from the other issues people bring (to counselling). Learning Difficulties cover a wide range of body processes from visual and listening problems to movement difficulties. There are few Counsellors that understand Learning Difficulties or even associate them with adults and children having behavioural problems.

The *Move to Learn* program is a great program for all ages. It has many advantages for the Counsellor.

• First, it can help the Counsellor to understand the person and their difficulties better. It has a large effect on improving their learning abilities.

• Second, the movement program is great for those with a variety of problems, including drug and alcohol abuse, mental illness and other issues.

People are often unable to exercise in a group setting due to their co-ordination difficulties and low self-esteem, as well as a lack of appropriate programs. The movement program offers these

Adults love it too!

people a simple program that will give them exercise and help their brain function. Mental diseases and Learning Difficulties are both neurological, so if the brain is being activated, the person doing the movements is going to benefit. Many counselling clients would benefit from participating in some form of movement before counselling so that they are able to remain focused during the counselling session.

I have lived in a Christian community called Obadiah for the last 10 years. The vision of Obadiah is to take care of those who need help. Over the years this has come to include those with mental problems, those with marriage problems, foster children, drug addicts, alcoholics, gamblers and many others. I have grown up having these people in my life and have learnt a wealth of information through them. I was recently introduced to the *Move to Learn* program and got excited about its vision. One of the most exciting things about the *Move to Learn* program is that it **can help people of all ages**. After reading Barbara's book and going to the 2005 Seminar I realized that 90% of the people we have here (at Obadiah) have Learning Difficulties and that there were things we could do to help them.

I began an adults' movement class this week with 5 adults. Stanley is in his 40s and suffering from schizophrenia, Dave is in his 30s and has significant mental difficulties. Annie is 35 and Carol is 40, both are recovering addicts with many problems, Maria is in her 30s and has many different mental and learning problems. I have started with them 10 minutes a day, five days a week. We do breathing first, and have been having lots of fun rolling and doing eye-tracking exercises.

There is a school on the property so we are using the hall in which to do the movement program. We bought plastic strips to put on the floor for stomach and hands and knee crawling. I have bought some spiky balls to use in the program. In the two weeks between the Seminar in Sydney and beginning the program with the adults I was worried they would find it boring. However, the first day they had so much fun they didn't want to leave and everyday they can't believe how quickly the 10 minutes go.

One of the early fruits of this program I have seen in this two weeks is the ability of the adults doing the program to leave their problems outside and be free (like children) to do their movements. They are so free in their laughter and enjoyment it is an absolute pleasure to teach them. Stanley has found that he has heaps more energy and is able to concentrate much better already. I have noticed that each of them is much more alert in their thinking. For the first time in most of their lives they are achieving things. The men in particular were never able to keep up with physical activities at school and now for the first time they are not only keeping up but succeeding and doing better than they ever thought possible. However, **my vision is to get more adults taking part in such a program whether they have obvious problems or not.**

10 Weeks Later

I have now been doing the movement program with the adults in my group for 10 weeks. Each one of them has benefited from the program. Sadly, I have had some decide not to keep going. Stanley in particular has stopped because he couldn't keep up with the changes in himself. I hope to continue working with Stanley (and some others) two to three days a week, to see if that pace is more beneficial for them. However, I don't see this as bad news, it is simply a learning curve. We know that the program works better if done five days a week but if someone is unable to cope with this, a less intense program might be just the key to help them.

With the adults that are still attending we are having a wonderful time. They know all the core exercises now and enjoy having me mix them up or go to stations for each different activity. Our school has graciously allowed me to use some of their equipment and so we have had lots of fun using a parachute, hoops, scoops and balls and skipping ropes. Recently I have been putting **classical music** on during crawling and this is Maria's favourite thing. Over the time I've had the program running I've had some people come and try it and then do it a couple of days a week. One of these people is Marion, a registered nurse with a 1 year old girl. Marion loves coming and is really enjoying the program and is delighted with the changes in herself. After a session she often says, "My mind feels so much clearer now, and I feel stimulated." Marion brings her 1 year old and I have been doing some exercises with her baby such as rolling her on a large ball and letting her play with scooter boards. She likes to watch the adults doing their exercises and the other day she got on the mat in the flip-flop position! She also is fascinated by eye tracking but finds it too hard yet!

The school at Obadiah is also involved in the Research project for *Move to Learn*. The kids are really enjoying the program. We are also learning which specialists to refer people to, which has been great as well. We recently sent a child to see a Behavioural Optometrist, who was able to prescribe a program to help. In the weeks since, we have noticed this child is a lot more comfortable, largely because she knows she is not dumb; there is actually something wrong, and something is being done to help her. **This program fills people with hope and gives them a vision to work towards.**

Movement can have a tremendous effect in counselling. One of the newer therapies in the counselling field is Body Focus Therapy. This focuses on the body and how it affects our emotions. "Introducing movement to rigid structure can kick loose hidden feelings. Through gentle inward attention and kinaesthetic awareness, feelings can be experienced" (Conger, 1994: 149). When our bodies are active it can often help our feelings to be expressed. Angry children made to sit in a corner simply stew on their anger; running and getting their body active helps dissipate the feelings. Then the child can sit still or do whatever discipline is desired. People with anger and anxiety problems are taught to notice when they feel the anger or anxiety rising, and to notice how their body responds. As an example an angry person often has clenched hands, tight muscles and bulging veins. As soon as they feel their muscles tightening they can (if they are aware of it) begin breathing exercises or movement programs to help control and limit that anger.

When counselling, clients can become very emotional, and a simple relaxation exercise done at the end or during the session can help calm their body, and not allow it to overwhelm them. I hope that

Move to Learn, together with counselling and help from other professionals, will give adults and children with Learning Difficulties the help they need and that we can bring knowledge and insight into an area which has been misunderstood for centuries.

In using the movement program in conjunction with counselling I am finding people have clearer thoughts, and are able to explain themselves better. It also gives them confidence that is spilling over into many different parts of their lives.

Chapter 7

Learning Difficulty Support Groups

Chapter 7

Learning Difficulty Support Groups

Who Can Help Support Those Struggling With Learning Difficulties?

The simple answer is that we can. You don't need to have a degree or a professional position. Anyone who has experienced the confusion of not knowing what to do about their own or their children's Learning Difficulties, who has experienced the isolation of being misunderstood, and the desperation of not being able to find the right help can offer support. Those who want to help others, and are prepared to be listed as a contact, are pivotal to the successful handling of the problem in any community. These people can effectively form a support group. Support groups can conveniently provide a place for searching parents, adults struggling with their own Learning Difficulties, and overloaded Teachers who ask, "Who can help me?"

Our Support Group at Oxford Falls, Sydney, NSW, Australia

Over the past years it has become increasingly obvious how important Support Groups are to people with problems who feel isolated and don't know where to turn for help. Most of the groups in NSW that I have been asked to speak to have been LD Support Groups, so I have been able to witness first hand the wonderful effect these groups are having in their communities, and I have also had an increasing number of enquiries from other communities that are wanting to start up their own support groups but are unsure of how to go about it. We thought that it might be helpful to start one up ourselves, so we could then pass along our experience and better understand some of the challenges that would be involved. There had been a lot of local interest, and we could certainly see the need for one in our area, but even so it seemed to take forever to get started.

We decided to meet on the last Thursday night of every month except December. For the first year and a bit we had between four to eight people come, including regular members. Most of the newcomers, especially the adult LDs, felt very embarrassed to walk in the door, and each meeting was largely taken up with attempts to make the newcomers feel welcome and give them a chance to unburden. We would spend our time sharing a bit about our children or our own learning problems so that the new member would be less anxious about sharing their story, and then gave them as much information as we could and recommendations of helpful local specialists who might be appropriate for them.

Although these newcomers nearly always opened up and changed during that first meeting in their attitude towards themselves - from feeling like a failure to being 'understood'- few of them came back.

This may have been merely because they had received all that they wanted at that point in time. Some of the simple things that were suggested, such as getting eyes checked or visiting an effective physical therapist, could likely have caused such a difference that the desperation that had driven them to the meeting in the first place was no longer so extreme.

Several of our newcomers were also adult students, struggling with their studies. We often advised that they should ask for the *ESL* notes (*English as a Second Language*) from the colleges they were attending. If they have these class notes, they don't have to take notes as they listen to each lecturer, which can be quite a challenge if they are unable to write at the same time as they are listening or if they struggle with poor handwriting. If those struggling students had been able to take our advice, they might have experienced a significant lifting of pressure and felt that they no longer needed support, but I had a nagging thought. Could we have done more?

It was time to evaluate.

We needed to find out some of the reasons why these newcomers hadn't returned, because we knew they couldn't possibly have learned everything they needed to know in one meeting.

With a little follow up, we discovered that in quite a number of cases they were still overwhelmed with the extra effort and work which all LDs and their families have to do to survive and were just too tired. They hadn't had time to learn enough about the root of their problems and were therefore still vulnerable to doubt and lack of direction.

Several of them were also still struggling with shyness. They hadn't been able to get to know any of us very well in only one session, and it was hard for them to get up the courage to return. This can be quite a problem for adult sufferers of LD who often battle a history of rejection and mishandling of social interactions. It became obvious that more in-between meeting support was needed to help them feel comfortable, such as practical help, a coffee together and an ear to listen over the phone. With a little encouragement, some returned, and we re-structured our meetings in an attempt to meet their need for more in-depth information.

We used *Help Your Child to Learn* in our meetings to practice our detective work of searching out the basic reasons behind each individual LD's problems, working initially through the list of questions on food intolerance, and then the questions in Chapter 5 on seeing a Chiropractor/Osteopath. We never made it to the movement questions in chapter 6 because we began to receive more and more newcomers and each new member needed to start at the beginning.

We had a lot of lively discussions but we didn't seem to be getting the whole job done.

Understanding at Last!

What Happened Next

In an attempt to give more individual attention and still be able to move on to practical help, we decided to restructure our meetings again, and divided them into 3 half hour sections. This structure has worked well for us, and is still used as a general guide.

First half hour: To enable everyone to be able to share, we decided to spend the first half hour in small groups with a leader for each group. New people are encouraged to give their details, and everyone is given a chance to talk in an intimate setting. Our male leader usually looks after the men who come. Since people are encouraged to attend 6 meetings, members also share what progress they have made between meetings.

Second half hour: Promptly at 8.00 we come together as a big group to learn something new about LD. Next month, for instance, we will show ten minutes of the DVD/video, *Move to Learn* and 15 minutes will be spent introducing a movement from the sequence on it. Everyone will be invited to get down on the floor to try it out. It is by 'doing' that we learn best, especially if we have some difficulties absorbing information through the eyes and/or ears. The whole group can participate in this process using the 'buddy system'.

Third half hour: The final part of the meeting gives people a chance to talk individually over coffee.

This format allows for quite a bit of freedom to further check out the DVD/video, to practice a particular movement a bit longer or just to talk. We encourage everyone to buy their own DVD/video to work with at home and then come back and show us their progress.

Since all of the members of the Support Group are connected in a personal way to Learning Difficulties, new members soon become old members, and very often they have a strong desire to help others. In this way, new leaders emerge and other groups start as word spreads and new people arrive in search of help.

The Perth (Australia) Experience

Winsome Richards from Perth (her personal story is in chapter 6) writes about her experiences.

"In 1983, together with a remedial Teacher from Boulder Junior Primary, I organized a meeting for the many parents we both knew who had children with learning disabilities. Our aim was to make parents aware of things they could do to help their children as young as possible, and give them knowledge as to how they can help with Learning Difficulties so they could avoid unintentionally aggravating the situation. From this meeting it was decided that a parent support group was needed and so the *Association in the Eastern Goldfields for Information and Support* was formed.

The base objectives of *A.E.G.I.S.* were:

• To assist parents whose children had difficulties with communication skills, listening, reading and writing.

• To enable parents to deal with their children's behavioural and emotional problems.

These objectives were achieved by:

• Support through sharing experiences.

• Providing a register of professional people who could assist with the many different childhood disabilities.

We organized guest speakers to conduct workshops and seminars for parents of all children in the Kalgoorlie/Boulder District (population approx 30,000) providing them with guidance in how best to help their children. The workshops were well attended and very much appreciated by the parents. These workshops and guest speakers covered conventional and alternative treatments for disabilities. Some of the topics and presenters were:

Physiotherapy, Speech and Occupational Therapy, Audiology, Diet, Behaviour, *Educational Guidance for Learning Difficulties*, *Systematic Training in Effective Parenting*, Chiropractic, Motor development, *Slow Learning Children's Group* (now known as *Active*), Workshop on the Grief Process, *S.P.E.L.D.*, *Meeralinga Children's Support Services*, *Touch for Health*, Educational Kinesiology, Scotopic Sensitivity.

Purposes of a Support Group

• To share information about the nature of LD.

• To encourage members to know there are solutions.

• To help them to follow their own 'gut' instincts.

• To help find the right professionals, in the right order.

• To create a 'safe' confidential place for group discussion.

• To keep an updated list of reachable professionals whom the support group members know have helped others in the past.

• To encourage newcomers to keep a record of their progress and all the reports they receive from professionals including school reports. They will be able to inspire others with these and they might be useful in obtaining funding or access to further educational support such as a 'writer' for examinations (see glossary).

Start One Yourself

Kerry Holt in Bendigo, Victoria, Australia recently wrote to us.

"I am planning to get a parent support group up and running in Bendigo (Australia) and any form of your input would be inspirational....I also plan to establish a resource library for parents to access easily."

Don't wait for 'someone else' to start a group in your local community. In many cases, there might not be anyone else, until you light the fire and get those around you excited about what can be done. As you get others excited, you will also find support for yourselves. And together, you can help to turn your community around.

Chapter 8

Research

Chapter 8

Research

My Mentor's Way of Working with her Students

When I first knew Sister Yvonne I used to marvel at the way she could quickly work out not only the areas of immaturity in her students, but also what she would do first to start their programs. If they were having trouble with reading she knew instantly that she needed to see if they were good listeners and then, checked if they had had their eyes and ears properly tested. Then their vestibular system. Was it mature and therefore accurate so that what they heard, felt and saw matched up?

Wow, it's a 'b'!

Sister would include in her students' programs a few punches at the punching bag to heighten messages from the muscles and she would bring out her sweet smelling herbs. The sense of smell is another basic, basic sense. Stimulating the sense of smell does wonders in normalising messages to the lower part of the brain because this sense goes directly, and thus more quickly, to the brain, to do its work of stimulation.

Sister's sweet smelling herbs

Sister's student would never ever have had such a good reading lesson before, and could actually succeed at everything in the lesson. Before many weeks, he or she was ready and willing to pick up a book and would soon be reading. No more unhappy struggling, because Sister knew where to start!

What has this to do with Research?

Sister and I worked separately with thousands of children over the past 35 years, but it didn't take that long for us to think that there must be a big loading of people with very immature sensory systems in the 'Learning Disabled' population. (We soon found that this same thing applied to adult LDs as to children.) Later on, all of the work at the Beach House (my centre at Manly, Australia) started with the need to mature these sensory systems and the brain first, or at least at the same time as we introduced appropriate remedial teaching.

Then I began to want to know exactly what proportion of the students coming to us for reading, spelling, number work and handwriting remediation had immature vestibular systems. So many of them were freaked out by, or craved, touch, or couldn't see the blackboard because of glare or couldn't make sense out of what was said in the classroom because of scrambled auditory connections and thus looked like 'dummies' – the very last thing that they actually were.

Up until this point I had dismissed the need for any kind of research. We all knew that what we were doing 'worked', and research was too hard for us to do. Nevertheless, I decided to put the results of our detailed full assessments on a database to help parents and Teachers at my seminars to understand about the huge incidence of neurological immaturity in our LD population. The more detailed results of this have been published in *Help Your Class to Learn* on pages 36 – 40.

The Survey of 187 of our Beach House Students

To prepare for this database, I recorded the results of the assessments of 187 students who had come to the Beach House in the early 1990s. Each of these children had been fully assessed by our Physiotherapist working in the paediatric area and a Resource or Special Needs Teacher experienced with LD children, in addition to other appropriate professionals outside our centre. We had looked at every sensory area, at their developmental stages, brain integration, academic achievement, social skills, sensitivities, diet, over and under activity, etc. Each area addressed was graded into one of three categories.

- **No significant problem** – at age level

- **Some problems** – not enough by itself to worry anyone but in conjunction with several other areas of development with 'some problems', it became difficult for that student.

- **Significant problems** – enough to make life and learning difficult in itself but not necessarily understood by anyone who didn't have a trained eye.

The results were not surprising to us, but whenever their significance was understood by a parent or a Teacher they were astonished. Immediately they would get to work doing movement sequences, and trampolining (if possible).

The summary of the information we collected in two of the necessary basic areas which are foundational for academic learning is as follows:

70% of the 187 children had a significantly immature **vestibular system** (see Glossary). A further 21% had a certain amount of immaturity, which left only **9%** of our 187 students with a mature vestibular system. We were beginning to see one reason why we had such good results at the Beach House. Nearly all our students used our trampoline and then got one for their own back yards. We had our students rolling on the floor and swinging in a net, hanging their heads over their beds at home, doing spelling words while on the top of the overhead ladder and scooter boarding down the ramp. All of these activities are designed to stimulate the vestibular system.

Another interesting statistic concerned the development **of a dominant side**. We thought back to 'the two generals' as discussed in the *Introduction* of this book, who each control a side of the body. At a certain point in people's lives one of the generals usually takes control of the other general and is the leader, making the side of the body he controls, the dominant or preferred side of the body, and the person becomes 'right or left handed', 'right or left footed', 'right or left eyed',

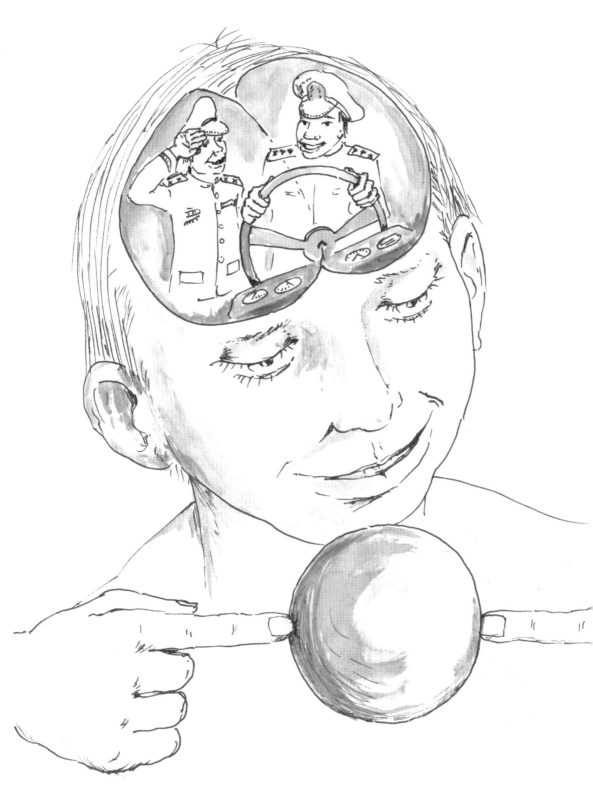

The Dominant General

etc. This usually happens at some time before the age of 7 or maybe 8 years. When this takeover by one of the generals doesn't actually happen and they both continue to try and control, there is a lot of confusion and inefficiency in performance and academic learning. Neither knows who is the boss! The person might be right handed, but left footed with a dominant left eye and a dominant right ear.

In my experience, however, there are a few people who function well using either side of the body as the dominant one. If their handwriting is easy and well-formed, with no LD struggles, we call them ambidextrous and wish we were like them.

The statistics that we have show us that a huge percentage of those who struggle to learn don't have a clearly dominant side and hate the stress of handwriting.

I began to be puzzled by something. How does all this compare with the population as a whole? What percentage of the world population has mixed dominance and/or an immature vestibular system? I had begun to have an interest in doing 'real research'.

Oxford Falls Grammar School

The next attempt that we had at collecting data was under the direction of Robyn Taylor, an Educational and Clinical Psychologist, at the school where I set up a movement program, combined with basic teaching of the 'three Rs'. This was described in chapter 1 of this book and was published in my third book, *Help Your Class to Learn*. At that time, in the early 1990s, I had accepted the belief that IQ (intelligence quotient) scores never changed and that they were a permanent record of a person's academic potential. Robyn's research severely challenged that belief.

We found that with the students who did our program, **their IQ scores rose significantly**, in a surprising number of cases. It was so encouraging to have some figures which showed us that movement was indeed the key to improved academic achievement. 'Research' was becoming a more pressing prospect.

The *Move to Learn* Sequences

These were formally packaged in 2001. A further interest in research was rekindled after we started getting such good feedback from classroom Teachers and parents who used the *Move to Learn* movement sequences. We wanted to know exactly how effective they were.

Had we thought of everything when we made the DVD?

- Enough activities to mature all the basic neurological areas?

- Enough wisdom when we said "no training was needed"?

- Enough time to attain students' readiness for the classroom?

We needed to find a researcher.

Dr. Christine Chapparo

My contacts brought me to Dr. Christine Chapparo, Senior Lecturer at the University of Sydney in the Department of Occupation and Leisure Sciences. I had heard that Chris had set up a highly thought of program involving movement in two public schools in Sydney, I asked her to share what she has done, for this book.

An Integrated School-Based Therapy Program for Language Impaired Childen *By Chris Chapparo*

The purpose of the project was to measure the outcomes that were achieved over two school terms. Academic performance, gross and fine motor performance and perception were measured. The background to this was that a request for Occupational Therapy assistance for children with specific language and communication difficulties was made to the School of Occupation and Leisure Sciences at the University of Sydney. They then developed a final year of specialised field work placement. The program targeted children K – 6 who were identified as having average or above average IQ, but significant language difficulties. In addition, the majority of children were identified by their Teachers as having problems with general organisation, planning, fine and gross motor abilities, developing relationships with peers and self-regulation of their behaviour. In other words, the majority had Learning Difficulties.

The program ran for eight weeks in each of the third and fourth terms in 2004. It focused on three areas: gross and fine motor skills and tool use (writing, cutting, pasting), and sensory processing and regulation. Fine motor intervention focused on hand and finger dexterity and strength. Pens, pencils and paper were the tools that were used. The whole of the classes were included every day in the activities and there were a number of individual sessions for those who needed extra help. As well, there were activities in the school hall aimed at developing tone, posture, balance and the ability to plan their own movement. The activities were graded from simple to complex as skills developed and could be used in the playground and Physical Education classes. Student therapists worked with specific children during class time on organisation, planning and regulating attention and behaviour.

This program was never put to the test of research but both schools are most anxious that the Occupational Therapy trainees will keep on coming. There were, however, some interesting statistical results.

Changes in Gross Motor Ability

Before and after a one term program, 53 children were tested on standard measures of muscle tone, co-contraction, movement control, balance, and integration of primitive reflexes. Results indicated a statistically significant difference in group performance ($p < 0.05$) on all measures except choreoathetosis (the ability to inhibit unconscious, unwanted finger movement). Teachers reported that the children had more controlled sitting positions during classroom work and that they were able to engage in physical games and sports with children from other classes within the school.

Changes In Fine Motor Ability, Handwriting and Tool Use

Using the Curtin University Handwriting Assessment, Handwriting Speed Test, measures of colouring and scissor use, 43 – 50 children were assessed before and after the program. Results indicated statistically significant improvements in group performance (p<0.05) on the following specific measures of hand function during class performance: bilateral use of both hands, joint laxity and stability of the fingers, hand strength, positioning of the head, neck and body during writing, forearm and wrist positioning during writing, maturity of pencil grasp, pressure during writing, improved letter formation, size, consistency and alignment during writing tasks. There was no significant improvement in group performance on measures of thumb movement and strength, or excessive index finger hyperextensibility during writing.

Teachers reported that, as a group, the children were able to organise their writing and fine motor tasks more independently within class, and were able to monitor and correct their own performance. Although not measured, Teachers reported an improved ability to attend to tasks; specifically, children were able to focus on parts of their work and maintain their attention for longer periods.

Change in Visual Perception

Using results from 40 children, we found that there was a significant difference in group performance on the Developmental Test of Visual Motor Integration (VMI) (p<0.05), with post test scores showing overall improvement. The most startling thing about this finding was that the researchers were not directly targeting concepts that related to visual perception per se, but rather, the functions that are thought to contribute to visual perception, such as learning where to look, learning how to look, learning how to scan, learning how to control posture and how to focus and maintain attention on a specific visual stimulus during class work.

Other Learning Through Movement Research in Australia

Training Classroom Teachers in Using Movement

Other research that is being thought about or done in Australia with the same knowledge of the value of movement comes from the state north of us, Queensland. Contributed by Maureen Hawke, Learning Connections, Brisbane, Queensland, Australia.

Learning Connections (established 1976) in Brisbane offers *Teacher Training* in programs for school age children as well as an *Early Years Program*. More than 1300 Teachers from over 300 schools have attended these training sessions since 2001.

Over the years Learning Connections has amassed large amounts of data from Teachers. This data shows that the *Learning Connections School Program* accelerates learning and improves behaviour. It provides children with the building blocks that are essential for successful learning and is essentially a sensory motor integration program.

Using specific exercises, children replicate the early movement experiences that are required to establish good building blocks or 'wiring' of the brain that is essential for efficient learning. These activities are carried out by the classroom Teacher. As well as the movement activities, Teachers are trained to use a range of specific learning strategies which, when used in conjunction with the *Learning Connections School Program*, are much more effective than traditional remedial work and tutoring alone. Improvements are not only seen in the children performing at below average levels but **in children of all abilities**. The underachiever may also be the child whose performance is average or above, and who is not giving their Teacher any cause for concern.

Teachers consistently report how much more focused their classes are after doing the *Learning Connections School Program* every morning, and that their teaching becomes more effective. In a controlled trial of 38 special needs children from years 3 to 7, there was a statistically significant improvement in reading accuracy of 8.8 months and an improvement in spelling age of 7.4 months after only 9 weeks of using the *Learning Connections School Program.*

Significant improvements in literacy and numeracy were documented by a South West Queensland school who won the 2005 Education Queensland Showcase Award for Excellence in early phase education. The Teachers attributed their success to having incorporated the *Learning Connections School Program,* along with other strategies, into the curriculum.

In the words of one Teacher using the program, "It works, use it daily" and from another, "I can definitely see that an improvement in the exercises is mirrored by an improvement in some areas of class work. This has been noted too many times to be deemed accidental. Learning Connections gives each child the opportunity to realise their true potential."

For further information, contact Learning Connections
www.learningconnections.com.au

My Own Current Pre-Research

Maureen Hawke's desire to do research to prove how essential specific movements are to academic learning has always excited me and I have admired her tireless, extremely effective training of hundreds of Teachers over the past few years. Properly conducted research is an essential requirement for broad based changes in long established practices. Unless those with the power to instigate change can be convinced of its necessity there is little hope of it happening. Properly conducted research is one of the most effective tools of persuasion.

I therefore decided to put more of my energy and support into research programs that would help in our battle for inclusion of movement programs into the basic curriculum of every school. I wanted to get involved with pre-research or preparation for research to determine how effective my nine sequenced movements are in preparing students for academic learning. We needed to know exactly what minimum number of activities will unlock a person's readiness for academic learning.

To this end, I partnered up with Dr. Chapparo to coordinate and assess a broader collection of information. I put the word out through my contacts to find Teachers and schools who would be willing to participate in this kind of research, and Dr. Chapparo agreed to interpret the collected results. The response was overwhelming and we had more people wanting to be involved than we could accommodate.

In the end, we settled on a broad cross section of Teachers working with children from pre-schools through to high school. In all, 264 students were involved from 13 schools. Four of the schools which asked to take part are based overseas – South Africa, Malaysia, New Zealand and the United States, and in Australia there were three government funded schools and ten private schools - seven from country areas and six from major cities.

Each Teacher was sent a copy of the *Move to Learn* DVD and asked to spend 10 minutes a day for 20 weeks if possible taking their class progressively through the movement sequences in the manner described in Chapter 5.

On top of that they were asked to fill out a Teachers' rating scale for each child every four weeks.

The rating scale had 13 items about the classroom performance of each of the students, including such things as posture, spacial layout, emotional control and completing work on time, that was designed to take roughly two minutes to complete.

This was then sent to Dr. Chapparo with a sample copy of each student's handwriting, spelling and other academic test results, and attendance record.

Results are still being assessed, but we are hopeful of not only some conclusive indicators of the effectiveness of these movements in enabling academic progress, but also of the spreading of excitement by the individual schools involved when they experience the results first hand.

This research is, of course, only the beginning. There is so much to learn, and all discoveries need to be properly evidenced, documented and presented. Fortunately there are many who feel the same excitement and vision that I do, for it will take many hands to complete this task.

Chapter 9

Additional Resources

Chapter 9

Additional Resources

9a Calming Students

Veronica pointed out to me, very wisely, that Teachers sometimes need more information on how to calm students than to stimulate them. She was very helpful in providing information about this with the aid of How does Your Engine Run? *By Williams, M.S. & Shellenberber, S (1994) if you want further details.* – Barbara Pheloung

Students who are constantly restless with frequent changes of posture, getting out of the chair, walking around the room, fidgeting, humming, smelling, chewing on clothing, can likely just be trying to feel 'right', more switched on and settled. Their bodies may need this extra movement and stimulation – usually more apparent in pre-school or the first year of school, but for some, this need stays on longer and it often doesn't do a lot for the other students around them. If a 'fidget toy' was put on the desk of each student it would be interesting to see which students fiddled and pulled on theirs during the lesson and which students weren't even tempted to touch them.

What about students who get visually distracted? Beautiful posters and paintings all over the walls of a classroom are not even noticed by some students but others are too distracted by this. Do we need to provide some calming time in a place with plain walls for these latter students?

There was a special school in Melbourne where students were allowed to get up, having asked for permission first, whenever they needed to. They could then proceed to go to the front to ask a Teacher a question or to the toilet or to get a book etc., but they were **allowed to go in whatever manner they wanted** – walking, cart wheels, crawling, upside down on hands or back flips. The amazing thing was, that during the two hours of our visit none of the students seemed to be distracted by what the others did. Some of the students only needed to walk, while others engaged in the most active and extreme ways of 'going'. They needed their own particular kind of movement, and when they got what they needed, they were able to settle back down to work.

What is the best way to deal with those who are seeking this extra activity? Since telling them to 'settle down and be quiet' is not really

Peace and Quiet at Last

Different Movement Needs

achievable, it is a relief for Teachers and parents to know that this very restlessness can be used to advantage. It is actually an expression of the child's body trying to get some kind of balance within the nervous system – a kind of self-stimulation. The body instinctively knows what it needs.

A pile of cushions in the corner of the classroom will attract some students who need to feel safe and comforted and cuddled and a suggested run around the school yard may do wonders for someone who just can't sit still for any length of time. A place to roll, or something to twirl or swing on, or even a few minutes of putting the head under the desk could settle a child who just can't get it together.

Calming music 'surrounding' the class has also been known to have remarkably settling effects.

Dealing with Refusal and Anger

There are also other physiologically based reactions which come from the autonomic nervous system that make Teachers' lives difficult. These are the automatic reactions of refusing to do something, running away from a situation or lashing back that some children display.

One very efficient method of dampening down or inhibiting this high level of arousal is to have the students do strong muscle work. Some activities can include:

- hands on side of chair and lifting body up and down

- wall push ups

- strongly squeezing toes inside shoes

- stretch and yawn

- squeeze shoulders

- fidget toys that encourage stretching, poking, pulling (See illustration Chapter 3)

- food that requires strong crunching e.g. carrots, celery

Wall Push-ups

• non-food items that are safe and clean to chew

• a selection of essences to smell

Further clues can be gained from obtaining information about the individual child. Likes and dislikes are not universal. Each child will have their own individual way of reacting to stimuli. It can be helpful to observe the child or to ask the parents questions about:

• What activities seem to interfere with, and what seem to help the child to work better?

• How long or how much of an activity is needed to benefit them?

• Is it swinging, spinning, squeezing behind furniture or under cushions?

• Is it listening to music?

165

• Does it affect the safety of the child, or the class?

Give the children information about themselves and their bodies, so that they can gain an understanding of 'who' they are and 'how' they function most effectively, and then try to raise their awareness of how they can fulfill their own needs without upsetting others.

9b Sound Therapy and Auditory Processing

by Veronica Steer, Occupational Therapist,
Sound Therapist and Kinesiologist

Poor Auditory Processing

After looking at diet and nutrition and doing the movement sequences, that may be sufficient for many students. If literacy gains are still limited, however, poor auditory processing may be one of the next things to investigate.

Research studies are finding that auditory processing difficulties are underlying 75% of literary and language difficulties. (Owens, 1999, from talk by Dr. Wayne Wilson, Audiologist and Researcher, Queensland, Australia, SAMONAS Conference, Sydney, October 2003)

Auditory processing, (for example, phonic decoding, which is attaching the right sounds to the right letters and in the right sequence), has a major influence on spelling, reading, comprehension and even mathematics. i.e. Accurate listening and understanding of concepts and set questions is obviously important for most learning. Poor auditory processing can severely hinder progress, and has also been seen to affect the student's ability to tolerate noise, cope with chatter in the classroom and the playground and even follow conversations. Difficulties in this area can affect relationships, self esteem, self expression, grammar, word finding and short term auditory memory.

Sound Therapy, undertaken by qualified practitioners, is one approach that has been shown to successfully address underlying auditory processing and has been repeatedly found to also improve visual processing and coordination.

Not Music Therapy

Sound Therapy is different from Music Therapy. In the former, quite specific technical changes have been made to enhance the therapeutic effect of the music. Up to 1,000 hours of production time can be involved in each minute of listening on some recordings. So Sound Therapy is not an ordinary listening experience but a therapy which is supervised by a qualified Sound Therapist (see websites below for practitioners).

Various forms have developed around the world since the pioneering work done by Alfred Tomatis, a French Ear, Nose and Throat Surgeon, in the 1940s.

Two home listening programs which use CDs are available: *SAMONAS Sound Therapy*, www.samonasaustralia.com and *The Listening Program,* www.advancedbrain.com. They involve daily listening to the CDs of 15 to 45 minutes depending on age and intensity needed, for approximately 6 months. This should be listened to on a good quality CD player with headphones **at home.** Each person has a program drawn up and reviewed to suit them. While listening, the student can be engaged in quiet play, reading, doing homework at bedtime or early morning. In this way it fits in with 'life' rather than imposing another learning /teaching demand.

The progress made by sound therapy, is measured in terms of changes in listening, attention, more settled behaviour, speed and effectiveness of auditory and visual processing, writing, bookwork presentation, coordination and greater verbal and social confidence. This, of course, flows on to reading and other academic work in due course.

It has been found that sound stimulation using the CDs provides efficient stimulation and maturation of the brain processing as it involves high frequencies of up to 30,000 hertz. Frequencies between 2,000 and 4,000 hertz are particularly important for understanding the speech sounds *p, b, k, d* and the higher frequencies of *f, s, sh, t, z.* The CDs incorporate sharp gradients as the music comes in and out, stimulates both ears with respect to timbre, pitch, volume, direction, immediate and distant space and sounds of nature. The music moves across the midline between L and R to aid integration of the two sides of the brain and their role in listening, speech, language and learning.

Listening Through the Bones

Bone conduction, involved in these Sound Therapy programs markedly increases their effectiveness (see the Australian SAMONAS website for gains achieved in literacy).

It is a normal and important part of hearing which is utilized in the sound therapies to tap into low frequency sounds/vibrations that are 'picked up' by the cochlear and the vestibular sensors, both of which are embedded in the bones of the skull. Bone conduction conveys the music directly to these sensors and their nerve pathways via the skull bones. This is particularly effective if there have been middle ear conditions affecting listening. It also taps into the very foundation pathways of sound being interpreted with the body senses.

The vestibular sense is well known to be closely tied into the proprioceptive (body position) sense and vision for balance, which is why children improve in a number of areas physically. Together these senses, and the connections they make, form important foundations for processing language and learning. Using bone and air conduction, therefore, has been found to make a major contribution to the processing of sound in our brains.

SAMONAS practitioners have collated the results obtained from children, adolescents and adults who have used the program over the past several years. The most recent 2004 results were presented at the SPELD NSW conference at Newcastle, Australia, 2004 and at the Inaugural Auditory Processing Seminar in Adelaide in 2004 and the Conference in Melbourne in early 2005.

These results indicated that participants were able to gain two to three years' improvement in reading and spelling after an average of six months of listening. Speed of intake of visual and auditory signals was recorded to have improved by two to three times in children, and even more in adults. Although not part of the tested outcomes, this would have meant that the participants would have experienced improvements in their ability to remember conversations and lessons and their understanding of what is read would have improved as well.

Music for the Classroom

Listening to music and learning a musical instrument is well supported in recent research to provide brain stimulation that provides benefits for learning, coordination, and 'healthy' emotional and immune systems (Jensen in *Music with the Brain in Mind*).

Although 'surround music' is not of the same intensity and nature as individual *Sound Therapy* using headphones, it can improve the concentration levels of the whole class.

Teachers can use a series of CDs called the *Sound Health Series* labelled for *Learning, Thinking, Concentration, Productivity, Relax and Creativity, Destress, Maximum Focus, Peak Performance.* www. advanced brain.com.

Other Sound Therapies

Tomatis Centres - the original Sound Therapy
www.tomatis-group.com/uk/frame.htm

Patricia & Rafaele Joudry Sound Therapy
www.soundtherapyinternational.com/

Auditory Integration Training Centres
www.dguyberard.com/

References:

Tallal, Paula (who has many research papers in the area of auditory processing and literacy). *Centre for Molecular and Behavioural Neuroscience*, Rutgers University, Newark, New Jersey 07102.

Warnke, Ralphe. *Central Processing and Automation Deficits as the Primary cause for reading and speaking difficulties. A Unifying hypothesis for Dysphasia and Dyslexia.*

C/-MediTECH Electronic GmbH
Langer Acker 7
D-30900 Wedemark

Steinbach, I. *SAMONAS Sound Therapy*; Kellinghusen, Germany. Techan Verlag, 1998.

Leeds, Joshua. *The Power of Sound.* Healing Arts Press, 2001.

Berard, Guy. *Hearing Equals Behaviour,* 2000.

Madaule, Paul. *When Hearing Comes Alive.*
The Listening Centre, 1994.

Tomatis, A. *The Conscious Ear.* Station Hill Press, 1992.

Jensen, E *Music with the Brain in Mind.* The Brain Store, San Deigo,CA, 2000.

Joudry, R. *Sound Therapy for the Walkman.* Steele and Steele, 1984.

9c Healing the Hurts

Everyone who has travelled the path of Learning Difficulties will have been deeply hurt at some time, and probably many times, in their lifetime. It is still so hard to identify someone who has LD and to understand that the neurological problems they are trying to deal with are causing symptoms which can be anti-social, isolating and hurtful to themselves and all those around them. Everyone is blamed – parents, peers, siblings, Teachers and especially people with LD themselves.

One young man told me about the constant bullying he received. He hadn't been a strong child nor could he do well in school or at games, like most of the others. At the end of one day a group of bullies tied him to the trunk of a tree without his clothes and just left him there until the janitor found him some time later. Being laughed at and made fun of was the hardest part to put up with, and eventually he came to believe that that was his lot in life – to provide amusement for others or to be 'the class clown' a term with which you may be familiar.

Over the last 35 years I have heard hundreds of similar stories. When a child like this then receives a look of despair from the Teacher and criticism at home he or she will be left in no doubt about their worthlessness. And the sad thing is that it is quite understandable that Teachers, parents and siblings would find much to criticise. Everyone around is challenged by the Learning Difficulties that someone might have. Homes have been broken up because of the stress and frustration and feelings of guilt. Teachers really struggle with students who are unable to concentrate or sit still, and disrupt other students who are able and anxious to learn. There are many victims of Learning Difficulties and nearly always there is need for healing.

The first job is to identify and remedy the basic causes of Learning Difficulties. That is why it is so important that everyone come to some understanding of these. The LD students themselves need to see that the poor functioning of their eyes, or the food additives which make them hyperactive, or the milk which is linked to their ear infections etc., are the real causes of their problems, and there is much that can be done to overcome them. Parents need to know that their children's learning problems are not the result of their poor parenting, and that they have done remarkably well just to have hung in there. Teachers need huge support and understanding. And everyone needs to know they are all on the same side – and that's **'the winning side'**.

Even when all this has started to happen and life is improving there may still be a lot of stress and hurt. Healing is needed, or the resulting garbage can be buried deep down inside of the sufferers seemingly forever. There is stress on stress. For example, the stress of a food not digesting properly, clumsiness, slow moving eyes, failure at school and then the ridicule of this failure and so on and on.

Applied Kinesiology

Veronica Steer, recommends Applied Kinesiology for addressing this stress.

She describes it as a non-invasive form of counselling – a gentle way to heal, using a holistic approach to improve learning skills and well-being. As a complementary therapy, it is claimed it can bring a person into balance by focusing on three aspects of human function which contribute to good health and learning.

- Structural (neurological, physical)

- Mental (emotional, psychological)

- Biochemical (nutritional, environmental)

People have reported significant changes in short periods of time, and a substantial reduction in stress.

We have also heard exciting endorsements of several of the other 'alternative' therapies available, and there are a wide variety of those: Acupuncture, Acupressure, Naturopathic and Chinese Medicine, Counselling, Support Groups and Therapeutic Massage to name a few. Many claim to help to improve physical, emotional and psychological health and practitioners can be found in an extraordinarily wide range of places. We are always keen to learn as much as we can about what is being offered.

Homeopathy

My younger daughter, Rennie, who has impressed me so much in the way she has been bringing up her 4 children, is very excited about the benefits of homeopathy. She is a firm believer in good nutrition and natural remedies as a recipe for good health. I asked her to write a few pearls for us because I know how closely good body health is tied to good emotional and mental health. She writes:

"Homeopathy was first developed nearly 200 years ago and was used extensively at the beginning of the last century until the discovery of penicillin and other wonder drugs. It is an extremely safe form of medicine, which both aids recovery from illness and maintains good health. What is fundamental is to choose a remedy that is as similar to the illness as possible. It is best to find a recommended homeopath with both experience and a good reputation."

Unfortunately, not all remedies offered are able to deliver the promised cure, but there are many that do. Sometimes our only protection against 'quacks' is to research the practitioner as thoroughly as possible and to rely on personal recommendation and proven results. Nothing can replace the value of an effective network to share information.

Christian Healing

From my own personal experience, healing does not always require expensive therapies. It can be found through the support of a friend, and can be as close to you as the prayer on your lips. There are different ways of healing people, and there is no doubt that some people have been given the 'gift of healing'. These healers, or the ones I have talked to, readily admit that they are only the 'vehicle' for the healing power that flows through them. They point back to the source of their power which comes from outside of them. Different people call this 'power' by different names. As a Christian I believe that the source of **all** healing power is from our Creator, God. This is the first port of call for me to go to when I need healing – both physical and emotional. And it is freely available to everyone.

www.elijahhouse.com.au A reference for Christian healing.

9d Food Journals

Michelle Learmouth, one of the pioneering classroom Teachers from Chapter 6 effectively made her students more aware of brain building eating by asking her students to keep a detailed journal of everything they ate for five days. Five of her students have given their permission to share these journals with others. – Barbara Pheloung

Food Journal

	Monday	Tuesday	Wednesday	Thursday
Breakfast	Rice bubbles/ milk	ot's milk	ot's milk	ot's milk
Morning tea	Vita wheats/vegemite milk	noodles muslie bar milk	pikelets/jam milk	crus pits dried apricots milk
Lunch	Nutella Sandwich Fruit juice	nutella Sandwich /Fruit juice	nutella Sandwich Fruit juice	hot dog Fruit juice chips
Afternoon tea	Donut water	Apple water	water Korean lollies	Donut rice cakes milk
Dinner	pasta/Bolognese Milk fruit / ice cream	prawns potato/Broccoli carrot/beans/ corn/Snow peas Milk fruit custard	fish potato/bracoli carrot/beans/ corn/zing Milk	Lamb chop potato/beans carrot/beans corn

Thursday

Breakfast: cereal-rice bubbles
        water
Morning tea: orange   water
Lunch: Puppodams   rice thins
with vegemite on them water
Afternoon tea: ice-cream biscuits
carrot milk
Dinner: Puppodums   meat with
mashed potato on top beans
    banana and coconut

Friday

Breakfast: cereal rice bubbles   water
Morning tea: Peanuts   water
Lunch: water 5 puppodums
rice thins with vegemite on them
Afternoon tea: ice-cream   nashi-
pear   water
Dinner: meat with mashed potato
on top water beans

Food Journal

Monday

Breakfast: porridge with milk and honey.

Recess: Orange

Lunch: Sandwich and nuts.

Snack: Jam and butter on toast.

dinner: tofu and rice   water

dessert: pear and pear juice

Tuesday
Breakfast: muesli Milk

Recess: Anzac Biscuit   water

Lunch: Sandwich nuts and orange

Snack: ice block Anzac Biscuit
Hot milo.

dinner: Salmon quiche water

dessert: fruit pie   water

food Journal

Monday

Breakfast: a bowl of corn frost cereal
and two cups of milk

Morning tea: tiny teddy and an apple.

Lunch: two tuna sushi rolls.

Snack: a piece of chocolate cake and
one a cup of milk

Dinner: Calamari spaghetti, broccoli salad, white
bait rice and two cups of milk.
fish

Tuesday

Break fast: two slices of bread with Nutella,
two slices of banana, one piece of orange and
two cups of milk.

Morning Tea: Three strips of battered
chicken, carrot slices and one slice of apple

lunch: One large white bait fish rice ball with
dried sea weed.

Snack: four tim tams, sea weed rice biscuits
three cups of organic apple juice.

dinner: meat lasagne, brocolli, white baitfish
three slices of bread and two glasses of
water.

Wednesday

Breakfast: two slices of bread with nutella, one piec of
Orange and one cup of milk.

Morning - tea: tiny teddys

lunch: white bait fish rice ball, brocolli, a piec of
apple and mini sausage.

Snack: One mini meat pie, one teri yaki chicken
sushi, two rice ball and one cup of tea

dinner: one bowl of teriyaki chicken,
baked potato and brocolli

Food Journey

	Monday	Tuesday	Wednesday	Thursday	Friday
breakfast	Milk	Milk and Sandwich	lots of fruite and milk	Milk	Milk
lunch	peanut butter Sandwich	butter in a Sandwich	two mandarines one apple and a sandwich	hot dogs chips and apple	butter Sandwich
Snakie	grapes and strawberris	two mandarins apple	three mandarine and a sandwich	ice cream	pan cakes
dinner	rice one eggs	rice and eggs and fish	noodles	eggs in rice	rice

eating healthy food is good for you

9e Getting Good Enough to Get on Teams

What can we do after the Move to Learn Sequences are Finished?

By Veronica Steer, Occupational Therapist

As Teachers and parents see their students becoming competent with the nine movement sequences, they ask, "What do we do next?" They can sense that some of the children are not ready yet to become part of a sports team or to keep up with others on the playground. They don't have the necessary skills, or the confidence, but it's obvious that they could greatly benefit from the experience.

The good news is that there are a number of things that can be done to reinforce the improvements started by the nine sequences and help to bridge the gap in ability between these children and their peers. These children usually need more work in the areas of:

Primitive reflex integration

Working two body sides together (bilateral integration)

Crossing the midline

Right and left brain integration

Sequencing and timing

Eye hand coordination for play and hand skills

Dexterity

Handwriting

On the Team - Hoop Catch

These things can be worked on by the simple inclusion of various directed activities (described below) into the learning schedule. Teachers may or may not choose to involve the whole class in this, particularly as some of the students will excel and the student who has difficulties can make an unfortunate comparison to others, but many of these activities are suitable and fun for the whole class, especially Dodge Ball and the dexterity exercises.

Preparation

Preparation is an important part of ALL the activities.

Sensory preparation, (done by shaking, rubbing, tapping, clapping, jumping), is important for 'waking up' the skin and muscles of fingers, arms and legs, in preparation for the actions. It increases alertness and anticipation and aids in **getting ready** instead of **just responding** - an important part of any ball type of activity.

Relaxation is also important. Breathing exercises, quick eye exercises and body stretching makes for a more supple and relaxed body for these activities. Some children become quite tense playing games because of their former failures, so relaxation is important to include.

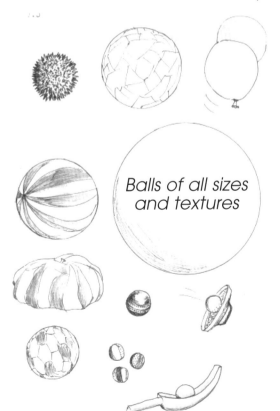

Balls of all sizes and textures

Ball Games

Many sports involve balls in some fashion or other, and many LD children are particularly weak in catching, throwing or tracking balls. These skills therefore need to be developed to allow these children to effectively participate.

It would be good to have a selection of balls that vary in size, speed of bounce, ease of catching and variety of texture for these activities so that the right one can be chosen for the degree of difficulty that a child is having.

First, develop all ball skills standing still. Having to move to catch puts much more demand on timing and judgment, and requires more layers of brain integration, which can only come after the basic skills have been mastered. Standing in a hoop or marked area can help centre some children.

*Bouncing between
Sending and Catching*

Secondly, encourage the student to visualise (with eyes closed) performance of the activity **before** they start. This can be done with every activity they learn until each movement becomes automatic.

Visualising

Thirdly, encourage the student to also verbalize the activity **while** they are doing it e.g. "bounce, clap, catch", and teach them to check their progress for themselves:

'Did it work?'

'Do I need to do it differently? E.g. softer, harder, higher, stand further away? or sideways?

Have them then repeat the activity and check again, but don't let them keep on doing something that is not working.

Finally, once they are feeling confident, you could suggest they try the activity blindfolded or with closed eyes, as a final challenge.

Basketball Drills

• Bounce drills –

Standing still – bounce and catch

Bounce and tap sequences

Step bounce catch, other foot, step bounce catch

Walk and bounce and catch

Run and bounce/dribble and catch

• Ball and wall drills –

Chalk or mark the line to stand at and to aim at.

Aiming at Targets

• Change the positions of the lines to increase the skill e.g. up to basketball ring height.

• Throw the ball on an angle to the wall e.g. over to the R and catch it by running over to the R.

Ball at angle to the wall

• Add different actions into the throw/bounce/catch/turn sequences.

• Ball and partner (Bounce to a partner, throw to a partner, throw to a partner while walking sideways.)

Large slow-bouncing ball

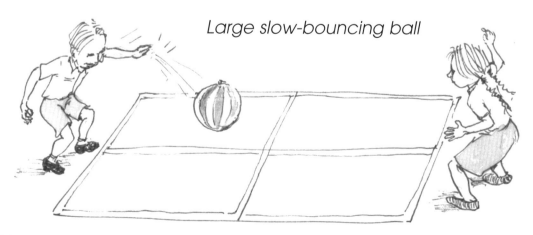

Dodge Ball

A group of children stand in a circle. One stands in the middle. The aim is to throw or bowl a soft ball underarm to hit the one in the middle below the knees.

If missed, it is then caught by the child opposite, who then takes his or her turn to try and hit the child in the middle, and so on.

The one in the middle has to turn, jump and move away as s/he closely monitors where the ball is around him or her. When s/he is hit, the one who hit him or her exchanges places and becomes the target.

Dodge Ball - A great game!

Bat and Ball

For developing pre-requisites for cricket, tennis, baseball, table tennis etc.

• Teach the correct body position for alignment to the ball and the swing through motion of the bat i.e. leading foot forward, the other back and sideways to the ball, not straight on. Standing side on, **front toe pointing in the direction of the target.** Perhaps you could have cut out foot prints positioned on the ground.

• Learn to aim and stroke first. A sheet can be pegged to a line (like a clothes line) to prevent balls from wandering too far.

*Learning to
Aim and Stroke*

• Bounce the ball with one hand and hit with the other.

• Aim to increase expectation of the number of times the ball is hit in a row.

• Teach 'back hand', and don't forget to change the feet and body position.

Each activity needs to be as successful as possible, so if a child is having difficulties, change the ball size, the speed of the bounce or the size of the target to reduce chance of failure. You can vary these activities to be directed at cricket or tennis, handball, baseball or table tennis on a table pushed against a wall.

You can also begin teaching games for students to play with friends at home and in the school yard. T-ball and adapted golf can be good as the ball is stationary when hitting.

T Ball

Football and Soccer

- Use alternate feet, not just one foot all the time.

- Kick the ball with one foot to the wall, and later to a partner.

- Learn to stop the ball with the out-turned side of the foot or placing the foot on top of the ball as it nears.

- The student kicks the ball as she weaves through a series of witches' hats or boxes.

Soccer trails

• Kick the ball in a scooping action to the wall at the right height to catch against the chest or to a partner to catch.

• Video Dad or a coach doing some soccer drills to reinforce visually how to develop skills.

Hands – Dexterity Exercises

Those with hand skill difficulties are going to be disadvantaged in many kinds of sports. Most of these children will also have sensory awareness difficulties and display difficulties with handwriting. Activities that develop dexterity can therefore show advantages in a number of fields, so go for it - use objects and activities that **stimulate the hands as much as possible.**

Pencil Gym

For developing a good pencil grip - teach students to tuck the 4th and 5th fingers into the palm, 'out of the way', then have them concentrate on getting the tripod grip fingers (thumb, index and middle fingers) to work together – perhaps put a sticker of a face on the tripod finger nails and make out the fingers are dancing. This is very good for developing the ability of these three fingers to work separately from the tucked in fourth and fifth fingers and is excellent preparation for using the pencil correctly.

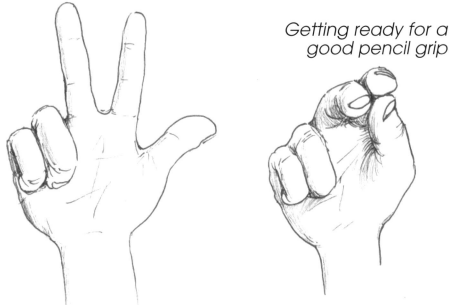

Getting ready for a good pencil grip

Another form of 'pencil gym' is to hold the pencil in the air and to use these three fingers to 'shuffle' the pencil up and down as the fingers work from one end of the pencil to the other.

Twirling the pencil with the 'writing fingers' in one direction and then the other also builds up the palm and finger muscles. Twirling the pencil with the other fingers can build up dexterity and strength for other clever hand activities as well. The next stage is to use both hands together with a pencil each.

Batons

A Baton can be also used for twirling. Being larger this can be done standing up and eventually walking around which will involve more brain pathways for co-ordination.

While we are suggesting activities about the Baton, can we also suggest using it to help to integrate some of the primitive reflexes that get in the way of eyes and hands working well together, for example the Asymmetrical Tonic Neck Reflex (see Chapter 5). The following is a good activity to help with this.

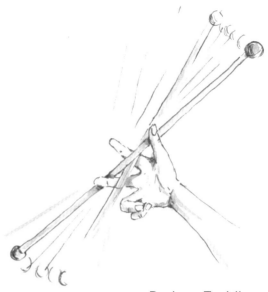

Baton Twirling

When standing, or with good straight sitting, the baton is held upright at chest level and the eyes keep watching as one hand slowly takes it out to the side in a full arm stretch. Keep looking while it is brought back to the chest and handed over to the other hand and then moved out to the other side and then back in. Three children can work together with one baton to be passed between them.

A variation can also be added to the middle of the sequence, when the baton is held directly in front at chest level. Take the baton in both hands and extend the arms to a full stretch out in front and then bring them back to the middle, or even to the face to help those who are scared of balls hitting them in the face (Moro Reflex). If necks and head are kept straight this also helps those who tend to bend over close to their writing (Symmetrical Tonic Neck Reflex).

Another variation is 'Baton Circles'. Here, two students stand back to back, and twist as they pass one baton across their body to the other student behind them. Both students twist to take and pass back, ensuring that they are crossing their midlines with their hands, and keeping their eyes on their baton. Then change direction. This further develops the segmental rolling. It develops rotation and the 'side-on stance' being developed in the bat and ball work.

Other Activities for Hands

• If you are teaching letter formation and fluency, don't forget to develop the sensory and visual memory. Try having the child attempt writing with his or her eyes closed.

*Writing with
your eyes closed*

• One hand coin tricks – hold a large coin between the little and ring fingers and then attempt to transfer it to the middle and ring fingers, and then the index and middle fingers and finally the index finger and the thumb. The other hand is not allowed to help.

• Marbles – any game of shooting or playing with marbles would be good for dexterity. 'Touchy' or sensitive feet and hands (left over primitive reflexes) also benefit from 'massaging' with marbles contained in a tray or box. Try picking up and moving the marbles from one finger to the other, or using the toes to pick up and drop marbles into containers or onto a target.

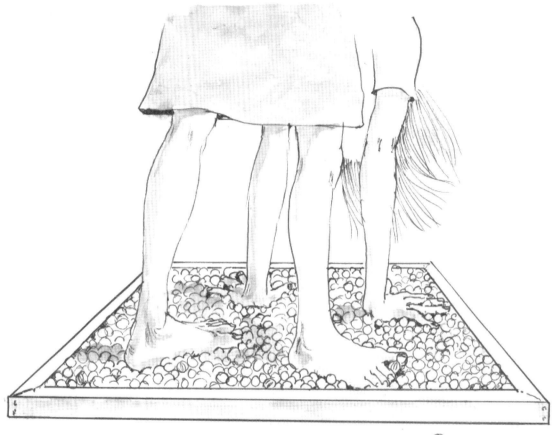

Hands and Feet in a tray of marbles

• Knucklebones - A child throws a knucklebone into the air and has to quickly pick up the others before catching it. There will be variations of this game in every country.

• Knucklebone juggling involves the transfer of a bone from the back of one hand to the palm of the same hand – back and forth. Using a small bean bag is an easier way to begin to learn this skill.

• Juggling - is fun as well as very beneficial for integration, eye-hand coordination and dexterity. Using one bean bag is a good way to start juggling, and it can be used to teach sequence and timing until it becomes easy to do and automatic. The children can then go on to

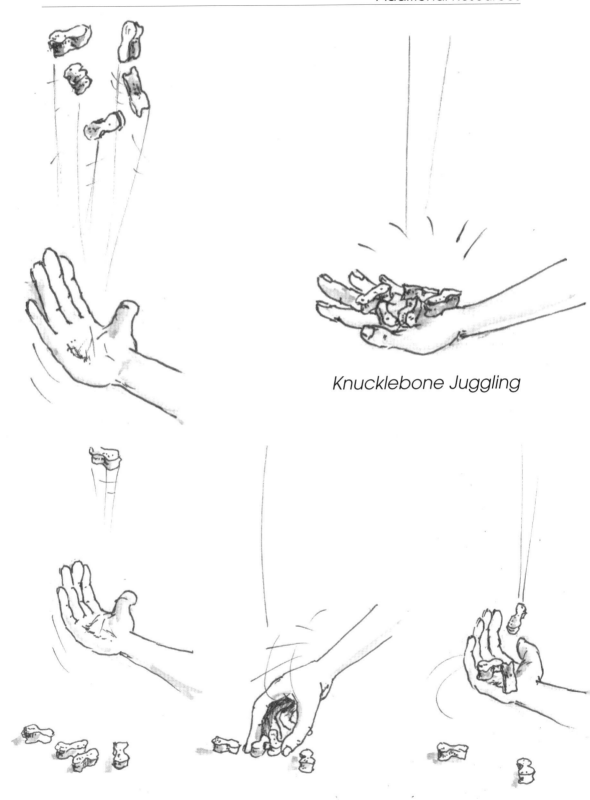

Knucklebone Juggling

Variation of Knucklebones

using two small palm sized bean bags or balls (Koosh) or rolled up socks that won't roll away when dropped.

• Cards - Shuffling cards is a great way to develop hand dexterity. Encourage the student to practice the slickest ways to shuffle cards to impress others.

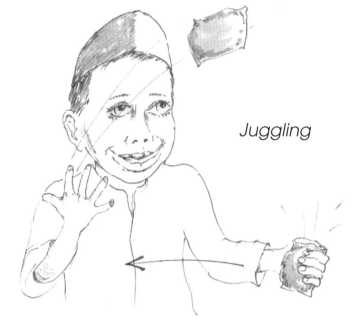

Juggling

• Then teach how **to deal**. To get the full benefits of integration, use both hands. You hold the pack in the non-dominant hand and release the top card one at a time with the thumb. The dominant hand takes each card and distributes them, always starting with the person on the dealer's left.

Handwriting

Standing at an upright board has been shown to benefit pencil grip and good wrist position for writing. A whiteboard station can easily be incorporated into the daily session. Watch out for the chemicals in some markers. Blackboards can be a little messy but may be readily available.

Teaching the Muscles How it Feels to Form Letters

Tracing over pre-drawn exercises, concentrating on matching size, evenness and length can be really helpful. Incorporate similar formations and commonly reversed letters, etc.

This is a particularly good activity to do with eyes open and then eyes closed.

For the older child the traditional cursive style can be modified to better suit those whose linked-print style does give them fluency. 'Cursive' enables less muscle strain than the stop-start, on-off the paper print style currently used in some states of Australia. Cursive writing needs to be introduced when brains are integrated.

Extended Wrist Tripod Grip

Practicing letters in their groupings, on large paper and with crayons or felt pens is not a new idea but important to use when re-educating handwriting.

Practicing in a tray of semolina or shaving cream takes pressure away from the pencil and paper approach and using relaxing background music can help to relieve the stress that many students have when writing. Again don't forget to practice with eyes open and eyes closed so that the visual and sensory feel of the letters becomes ingrained.

These, of course, are not the only activities that can be helpful. Any activities that encourage primitive reflex integration or bilateral integration, or help to develop the student's sense of sequencing and timing, their eye hand coordination or their dexterity are likely to ultimately help that child to improve their performance both in sports and in the classroom.

Shuffling Cards the Professional way

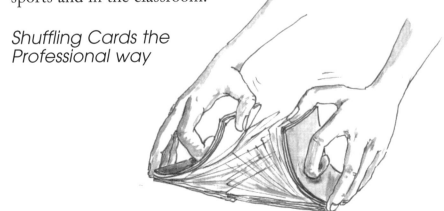

Preparing for a Social Life

Ballroom dancing is a fun way to improve co-ordination and flexibility. It is also a good way for teenagers to learn how to interact acceptably with the opposite sex.

*Preparing for
the School Dance*

The following web reference is very helpful for Schools dedicated to further program development.

Personal Development, Health and Physical Education
(K-Year 6/ Primary School)

http://www.bosnsw-k6.nsw.edu.au/pdhpe/pdhpe_index.html

This has excellent information regarding Syllabus, Resource List, Parent Guide, Principal's package and Modules.

9f How to Survive the Playground

Jacqueline Lee, Acting Principal.

• Born in country NSW, Australia, and always had a strong desire to work with country students.

• University educated through Australian Catholic University. Have also completed my Master of Leadership and Management in Education (with high distinction)

• Worked in a number of schools as a classroom Teacher (have taught everything from Kinder through to Year 6), including a school with an enrolment of 50% indigenous students.

• Held Executive positions including Coordinator, Assistant Principal and now Acting Principal.

• Passionate about the education of all students, particularly those with special needs in our mainstream schools.

• Passionate about professional development and, in particular, my own need to continually grow and evolve along with current research.

• Passionate about the link between myself as an educator, the students, and their families, as I believe that unless this link is effective and positive, children will not achieve their potential.

Take care!

The Situation of LD Students

When most people think about children with Learning Difficulties, they think about meeting the child's needs within the classroom setting. This setting is quite structured and protected. In a well managed and caring classroom it is quite easy for our LD children to feel safe and secure.

Then, at least twice a day, they are told to 'play'. They are thrown into a space that usually requires children to be quite independent yet able to socialise, able to plan their play, and be physically adept.

The Physical Needs of Many of Those Who Still Have Learning Difficulties

Let's think about the physical needs of many of our children with Learning Difficulties. They have **poor**:

- integration of the two sides of their body

- integration of primitive reflexes that leads to poor gross motor and fine motor skills

- hand-eye coordination

- motor planning and thus often don't enjoy playground activity

- spatial awareness

- visual and auditory processing skills, particularly when trying to discriminate sounds and visual information from background information

- social skills, particularly making and keeping friends

Emotional Development of LD Children

Forcing children with LD into the playground without support often leads to feelings of:

- Poor confidence, leading to low self-esteem

- Inadequacy

- Withdrawal, and often not wanting to come to school

• Poor social skills

• Frustration and even aggression or other non acceptable behaviours

All of these can lead to mental health issues such as depression.

How are these children supposed to go and 'play' and socialize with this level of difficulty?

What can Teachers do to Help These Children?

• The *Move to Learn* program needs to be on the curriculum of every classroom until it is successfully completed. It needs to be followed exactly and done every school day for 15 to 20 minutes.

• Communication programs are also necessary to assist and develop better communication skills. The need to teach and model skills that assist LD students to choose to act in a way that is socially appropriate, and help them to learn about cause and consequence, particularly in relation to their demonstrated playground behaviours. They need to learn what to do if the social situation changes, e.g. "we are playing cricket today, not soccer as usual" and how to socialize with a group.

• Teachers can use their Physical Education, or other appropriate time, to teach games and skills that can be used in the playground. Specifically teaching skipping, or soccer skills can be extremely useful for all children **when it is done after the *Move to Learn* movement sequences have been nearly completed.** LD children then know how to participate in these games. It also assists with their overall skill development.

• Clubs are another useful lunchtime activity. They can be focused on areas that the curriculum may not cover such as chess, gardening, craft, even French knitting! Not only do these clubs provide another option for LD children at lunch time, they also provide an avenue in which these children can succeed. It is particularly important

*Playground Equipment
to Develop Basic Skills*

for them to succeed in front of their peers, and receive positive feedback from both them and their club leader.

• Learning Support Assistants, or a designated Teacher, can spend time working in the playground with the specific purpose of assisting LD students. They can also act as an observer for older children and then conference with them immediately after play time. This conference can focus on what worked well, and where improvements can be made. It should always have a positive end so that LD children are comfortable and confident to approach the next play time.

• Varied areas in the playground for different needs are important for schools to consider. There should be areas that are shaded for quiet games, room for team sports, seating in which small groups can chat, safe 'digging' spots, places with equipment that promotes gross motor development and also a small hard surface games area for activities such as handball and hopscotch.

• Playground equipment is a wonderful tool for LD students if it provides opportunities to strengthen their basic skills so they can later join teams or play games and be able to keep up with the others. Such equipment could include a rotating barrel, monkey bars (that have a wide launching and landing panel at an appropriate height), climbing frame etc.

• Sporting equipment that is available for all children to use is crucial. Many confident children bring in their own equipment, but LD children often do not feel able to follow this lead. Having equipment available for children to use is important for equity between students and for encouraging all to become involved in sporting activities. Looking after this equipment and/or distributing and collecting it, could also be an area where these children shine.

• We find many of our LD children in the Computer room and Library. These places can provide a place of refuge for our LD children at playtime. An effective Librarian can facilitate activities that can not only stimulate young minds, but also lead to a sense of success. Some LD children enjoy assisting the Librarian as a Library monitor, and others excel in the area of technology. We have given them the role of being Computer Assistant, and they spend some of their playtime assisting other students in the Computer Room.

A happy and safe playground is the result of such strategies being utilized. Instead of having a child who bumps into other children on the playground, who is pushed aside by others, is awkward and clumsy, laughed at and withdrawn or on the other hand extremely aggressive, you can have a confident and developing playground user. Of course, it is essential to have all staff well aware of these students, their needs and the strategies developed to assist them. The playground can go from being a nightmare to a dream!

Do It Yourself
Playground Equipment

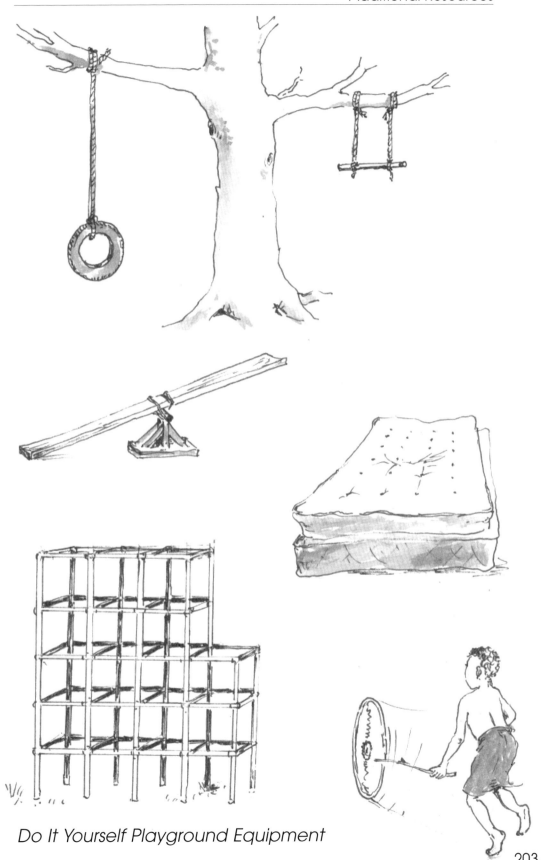

Do It Yourself Playground Equipment

9g Parental Help with Movement Program

Sue McKay, a Teacher who has been using a movement program in her school for 3 years, has developed some strategies to get the assistance she needs. The following is an example of her letters to parents. – Barbara Pheloung

---

Dear Parents,

We are desperate!!!!!

For *Move to Learn* to continue this year, parents and/or community members are desperately needed. Your commitment is for one hour once a week for Terms 2 and 3.

Move to Learn is a fitness program aimed at developing co-ordination and gross motor skills. All students in Kinder, Years 1 and 2 run through a circuit of activities across four mornings of the week.

Parents are stationed at each of the circuit activities to assist and direct children. No previous experience necessary! If you are able to help, even if it is just for Term 2, please return the section at the bottom of the note to the office ASAP.

The roster of classes is listed below for your information:

9.45am – 2N Miss Noble

10.00am – 2C Mrs Clack

10.15am – 1GB Mrs Gornall/Bird

10.30am – 1S Mrs Smith

10.45am – KW Mrs Wickham

11.00am – KN Mrs Nicholls

Thanks,

Sue Mackay

Move to Learn

I am able to help with *Move to Learn*   Yes   No

Please tick the time slot which suits you best:

Monday	Tuesday	Wednesday	Thursday
9.30 – 10.30	9.30 – 10.30	9.30 – 10.30	9.30 – 10.30
10.30 – 11.30	10.30 – 11.30	10.30 – 11.30	10.30 – 11.30

Name:..

9h Applying for Funding for Early Assessment

Winsome Richards who shared her experiences with movement and learning in Chapter 6a also sent this along for this book. She has always seen the need for early assessment as has Pye Twaddell so that children can be ready to learn before they start failing. – Barbara Pheloung

Proposal for South Kalgoorlie Australia, Pre-Primary in 1998

We have five Pre-Primary centres with positions for approximately 129 children.

I would like to see South Kalgoorlie used as a Pilot School and have:

1. Every child assessed in 2nd term to see if there are any delays or problems in:

> Speech and language skills
>
> Motor and physical skills
>
> Laterality and co-ordination
>
> Eye tracking

2. A program developed to begin early intervention for those children considered to be at risk.

3. The program commenced as soon as possible after assessment in second term.

4. The parents encouraged in learning how to help their child both in the home and at school.

How could this be implemented?

1. The Teacher could do the initial assessment with assistance from myself. I would be able to show her how to test the areas she is not sure about.

To do this I would have to spend the morning session for one week with each Teacher and her class. This could be achieved by me swapping with the assistant from each classroom.

2. The program could be developed with co-operation from the Speech Co-ordinator from the Goldfields District Education Office, Kalgoorlie Regional Hospital and the Primary School. The Occupational Therapist would need to be involved.

3. Every morning, children from each class assessed as being at risk could be worked with in small groups or individually if necessary. One assistant could implement this early intervention program so that all children are helped in a consistent manner.

4. Parent education could be accomplished through communication, books, workshops, handouts and guest speakers from the various professions involved with children and their development.

How could this be funded with the least cost possible?

If I were to implement this program under the direction of the Teacher from each class, another assistant could replace my position. The cost for a Level 1 assistant for approximately 24 weeks would be less than $4,000.

Winsome Richards

9i Australian Dirty Dozen Additives

Be wise and protect your family from the additives listed below.

By Sue Dengate, author of the Fed Up series and the Failsafe Cookbook, published by Random House. For more information see www. fedupwithfoodadditives.info – Barbara Pheloung

1. Artificial colours are widely used in confectionery, drinks and other foods. They can be listed by name or number: 102 tartrazine,104 quinoline yellow, 107 yellow 2G, 110 sunset yellow, 122 azorubine, carmoisine,123 amaranth, 124 ponceau, brilliant scarlet, 127 erythrosine, 128 red 2G, 129 allura, red, 132 indigotine or indigo carmine, 133 brilliant blue, 142 food green, 151 brilliant black, 155 chocolate brown.

2. Natural colour 160b annatto extracts is the only natural colour that affects some children as badly as artificial colours. It is found in ice cream, yoghurts and other foods.

3. 200-203 sorbate preservatives are found in drinks, dips and other foods.

4. 210-219 benzoate preservatives are found in drinks, fruit toppings, syrups and medications.

5. 220-228 sulphur dioxide and other sulphite preservatives are found in dried fruit, fruit drinks, sausages, medications and a wide range of foods and drinks. Sulphites can cause any of the full range of intolerance reactions but are especially associated with asthma.

6. 249-252 nitrate and nitrite preservatives are found in ham, bacon and deli meats.

7. 280-283 propionate preservatives are found in bread, buns, crumpets, cakes and other bakery products. Whey powder used in bakery products can be cultured with propionibacteria which is a natural method of using propionate preservatives while claiming 'no added preservatives'.

8. 310-312 gallate antioxidants used as preservatives in fats, vegetable oils, margarines. Unlike natural antioxidants such as Vitamins C or E, synthetic antioxidants can cause the full range of nasty side effects. See also 319-321.

9. 319-321 synthetic antioxidants TBHQ, BHA and BHT, as above. Antioxidants may be unlisted if used in an oil that forms less than 5 per cent of a product such as soymilk or frozen chips and they no longer act as a preservative. However, the unlisted dose can be enough to affect a child particularly if consumed frequently.

10. The '600 numbers' flavour enhancers including MSG 621, Ribonucleotides 635 and others in seasoned chicken, flavoured biscuits, chips, snacks, soups, sauces, stock cubes and takeaways. HVP, HPP (hydrolysed vegetable or plant protein) and yeast extract are natural forms of MSG. Ribonucleotides can cause any of the full range of food intolerance reactions but are especially associated with itchy skin rashes and swelling of the lips, tongue and eyes.

11. Sugar free sweeteners in sugar free foods, drinks, chewing gum and medications including the polyols (420 sorbitol, 421 mannitol, 422 glycerol, 965 maltitol and 967 xylitol) that can cause stomach discomfort and bloating through to excruciating stomach pains and sudden diarrhoea even at low doses in some consumers. There are some serious concerns in the EU regarding the safety of 951 aspartame.

12. Flavours. There are thousands of unregulated flavours. No code numbers are required as they are considered to be trade secrets.

Nasty natural chemicals. Children who react to artificial colours can be affected just as badly by natural chemicals called salicylates and amines in a range of fruit and vegetables especially citrus and tomatoes. Some families see an improvement by reducing their additive intake, while others achieve much better results with a three week dietitian-supervised trial of a diet, free of additives and low in salicylates and amines.

9j Quick Functional Vision Screening for Teachers

by Sue Larter, BOptom, MSc, FACBO, FCOVD

Observation is one of the best clues to potential vision problems: if you notice a child blinking excessively, squinting, rubbing their eyes, tilting their head; or if they complain of headaches, blurred vision, sore eyes; or if they lose their place when reading, copy inaccurately, have poor comprehension or poorly spaced handwriting and are still reversing letters or numerals after age 8, these clues all suggest that a thorough visual assessment is indicated.

If you suspect a vision problem the following two tests may help you decide:

Convergence test – Relevant for all school-aged children

To be alerted as to whether a student's eyes work well together, hold a small, detailed object (eg pen tip held vertically) about 30cm in front of child's nose. Instruct the child to carefully watch the point of the pen. Slowly advance the pen directly towards the child's nose, asking the child to try to keep the pen looking like one, but to let you know if they see two. Observe the child's eyes. Both eyes should move in towards the nose equally and smoothly. Repeat your observation at least three times to ensure that there is no break-down in function over time.

If the child cannot converge to 6cm from their nose, or if you notice one or other eye swing out as the pen comes closer, referral is indicated for a thorough eye examination.

Eye Movements (Tracking) – *Relevant for all children 6 years+*

Again hold a small detailed object about 30cm in front of child's nose. Instruct the child to "carefully watch the point of the pen and follow it just with your eyes". Slowly move the pen tip in a circular motion, no wider than shoulder width and no higher than the forehead. Observe the child's eye movements as the pen makes 2 full circles clockwise and two anti-clockwise.

If the child cannot follow the target smoothly with both eyes, or is distracted by other visual stimuli in the background, or uses head movements instead of eye movements, referral is indicated for a thorough eye examination.

For further information about Vision and Learning,
see www.acbo.org.au

9k Ready for School?

The Learning Place Kindergarten Screening

How do parents and Teachers know that the adorable little flower that comes to school on their very first day is really ready to keep on blooming? Are they ready to make the most out of 'this new world'? Dr. Pye Twaddell has spent years of conscientious study and work with preschool, kindergarten and primary school children, to devise a way for us to answer that question. The result is an Early Kindergarten Screening Assessment which can be given to a whole class in one morning by the classroom Teacher and a few helpers. It then only needs to be scored by the classroom Teacher.

The results help identify children who:

- *are developing typically*

- *may need more practice on foundation skills*

- *may need direct intervention*

- *may be potentially gifted*

- *may have a combination of possibilities*

I personally loved watching her video of so many children during actual screening sessions in their own local school environments. The familiar surroundings encouraged children's natural enthusiasm even if their skills were not all there yet. – Barbara Pheloung

Developed and validated by:
Pye Twaddell, BA Brown U., MA.UNH, PhD (Education) Syd.

Screening Kindergarten Children (5/6 year olds)

The intent of screening kindergarten children at school entry is to identify and accommodate their developmental and learning needs to inform instruction and direct intervention. Results from *The Learning Place Kindergarten Screening Instrument* give standardised quantitative information, (e.g., percentiles, means and standard information) and unique child qualitative information about the spontaneous independent functioning of each child's abilities, skills and understanding of basic concepts, by observing their performance of typical kindergarten 5 year old tasks with their peers.

The Kindergarten Screening Instrument was validated over 3 years in doctoral research at the University of Sydney with 3 separate groups of children. This inquiry focused on the issues associated with screening kindergarten children on entry to formal school, evaluating function during actual task performance as opposed to clinical assessment, and producing standard scores for valid comparisons.

The combined Samples totalled 776 children screened early in the school year and 833 children screened late in the year from 15 city, suburban and rural NSW schools. Evidence was obtained of internal consistency and the reliability of scores over time and across contexts and evaluators. The full scale Alpha reliability coefficient is .91. Scores are tabled for the Combined Samples and by age, gender and time of year. Among the standard scores are high and low target scores to further help identify those children who may be significantly at risk or perhaps more talented.

The research demonstrated that in-school kindergarten screening can fairly evaluate and identify the developmental and learning needs of each child screened and differences among the children, and that instructional adjustments based upon assessed needs have positive outcomes for children.

Assessment Categories are Outside Motor, Fine Motor, Oral Language, Paper/Pencil and Reasoning, and four Personal Characteristics such as attention. *The Kindergarten Screening Instrument* is: cost effective; easy to administer, score and interpret by classroom Teachers; and can be completed for a whole class together in about two hours, (despite the children's range of age and other diversities).

The Screening Manual contains: in-service information, assessment administration and scoring criteria, masters for all necessary forms, e.g., checklists, worksheets and records, hands-on practice scoring written work and completing records, reference tables, and summary of validation research.

The 38 minute in-service video shows procedure and the responses of many children during actual screening sessions in schools.

For further information contact Pye Twaddell at:
thelearn@bigpond.net.au

91 Signs to Look for Before the Third Birthday

MY CHILD'S SO BRIGHT BUT….. has s/he gone through the developmental stages of 0 to 3 year olds?

By Barbara Pheloung, *Move to Learn*

The daughter of a good friend of mine called me the other day from Melbourne. "Cassia isn't crawling, she's shuffling around on her bottom. Dad said to call you. Is crawling really important?"

"Tell me, Alex, exactly what is Cassia doing? How old is she again?"

"She's nearly 11 months. She sits on her bottom and one foot comes forward, it presses in to the floor and she leans on her opposite arm, propels herself in a semi-circular movement, sliding her bottom and other leg (which is folded under her) across the floor. She then puts her foot forward and does it again – a half drag bottom shuffle, I guess. I'm not sure how to describe it exactly, but it's very awkward looking," she said hesitatingly.

"Alex, did Cassia go through the rocking stage like your first daughter? I can remember your Dad telling me about Juno's rocking back and forth on her hands and knees for at least a couple of weeks before crawling."

"No, Barb……..Cassia isn't as strong as Juno…….but she's very bright. It's almost as if her little body can't quite keep up with her big mind."

"It's okay, Alex", I said "You will just need to take her back a few steps in her development and teach her what to do. Maybe she didn't even roll correctly. When you've checked that out, then get her on her tummy a few times each day, and all of you, even her Dad when he can, and particularly her big sister, get down on the floor with her and move around like commandos. Dig or press your hands and feet into the floor and wriggle and have races. Have fun!"

"But she might want to keep sitting up!"

Quickly I said, "Alex, that's okay. Keep playfully swooping her up and put her back on her stomach, as much as she can tolerate, and you keep wiggling and moving around on your stomach as well. Then gradually you start getting up into the hands and knees position. Show Cassia where her knees are. Rub them. She may not know that she has knees for kneeling. As each day passes, with plenty of this floor work, she will gain the strength to raise herself to her hands and knees. It is essential that she does this before anything else."

"Didn't your Dad tell you about my DVD/video?" I then asked Alex. "This will show you how to re-teach Cassia what she has missed."

"We haven't got that yet but he brought us your first book."

If there are Learning Difficulties in the family or indications of a general delay in some areas of a child's development, it is important that parents are aware of what to look for in those first 3 years of life. This is the easiest time to 'catch up' or 'fill in the gaps'. In the hundreds of children we have seen who are struggling at school, without exception, they all had experienced some of the developmental immaturities or missed out on some of the experiences listed below. Many of these children, like members of my own family, got through school reasonably well but if we had only known then what we know now it would have been so much easier for them.

Experiences Needed by Children by their Third Birthday

All children should have:

• Started their floor time on their backs because they are not strong enough to hold up their heads. In this position they can be encouraged to get to know their hands and feet. With their eyes looking at their hands and feet, at their midline, this is the beginning of integration. Parents can be encouraged to come close and chat with them while they are in this attentive position. This is their brain-building floor time separate from 'sleeping time'.

Research has shown that **sleeping on the stomach** increases the incidence of Sudden Infant Death Syndrome (SIDS).

• Lots of time on the floor on the stomach. This should increase as they gain the strength to hold up their heads. They can be encouraged little by little, by parents being on the floor playing, imitating and rolling around with them. Eventually they will start to move around on their stomachs, to get something they see or to be near Mum, who could be rolling near them.

• The opportunity to roll, which is the next developmental building block. They need to roll onto the back, onto the front, over and over. Eventually they will learn to lead by the eyes so that it can be done in a straight line, and flexibly as well. (If they don't end up doing this easily or well, follow the instructions on the DVD/video *Move to Learn*.

• The experience of getting onto their hands and knees as Cassia's Mum is about to show her to do.

• The opportunity to start to move around on their stomachs, to get something they see or to be near Dad, who might be stomach crawling near them.

• The experience of rocking rhythmically backwards and forwards on hands and knees but not going anywhere. This must not be missed. Your babies will know when they have had enough of this, because it is at that point they will start to crawl.

• Six months of crawling/creeping on hands and knees, even if they also start walking in the middle of it.

• The experience of having a comfortable daily routine where children come to expect what is going to happen next. For example a family sitting around at mealtimes, practicing good manners and learning to take turns talking.

• Investigated every safe available cupboard.

• Experienced 'safe falling' without undue fear because they have had the opportunity to learn how to fall without hurting themselves.

• Experienced as many different, safe smells and tastes as possible.

• Been allowed to put everything that won't harm them in their mouths to investigate. (Don't worry about the odd fly).

• Been able to touch and handle many things with different textures that have been left within reach.

• Had lots of hugs.

• Been 'rough housed' (appropriately thrown around by dad or a near relative)

• Been able to experience as much as possible the motion and changed positions of swinging, sliding, twirling and hanging upside down.

• Been listened to and talked to forever and ever.

• Been read to even though they have had so much that they can correct your omissions and mistakes.

• Learned how to bring their thoughts into a simple sentence.

• Have experienced Mum rhythmically counting their steps as they walk, or jump or move blocks or put dolls to bed…. "One, two, three, etc."

• The ability, by three years of age, to unconsciously reach across the middle of the body while playing, instead of passing something from one hand to the other.

Things to Remember

It is not a race

It is not as important when children reach a certain stage in their development as long as they go through each stage.

Each stage can be learnt, if necessary i.e if children don't roll in the right way they can be taught.

Every child has certain brain building rights

- To have good simple food

- To get dirty a lot

- To continually explore

- To learn to fall safely

- To be noisy at times

- To talk and be listened to – within limits

- To have carers who get down on the floor and learn from their babies how to play

Each child is differently gifted

Parents instinctively know the potential of their children but sometimes there is so much stress in a family for various reasons, including Learning Difficulties, that this stress masks the children's true potential. We all need to learn to read the behaviour of the children who mystify us.

Children never fail

Those who don't do things well or who 'muck up' have probably been given something too hard or too easy for them to do. This is usually just lack of knowledge on the carers' part.

New knowledge and confirmation of what we already know of a child's development between 0 to 3 years can be gained.

Move to Learn books and DVD/video have put together the knowledge and experience of Australian professionals who are among the best in the world in the field of child development. They can be accessed through www.movetolearn.net.

The late Dr. M.L. Sheil and her sister, Margaret Sasse of Kindy Gymbaroo fame produced the excellent series of videos on the stages of development in the pre-school years: *The Importance of Being an Infant* (revised 2006) and The *Importance of Being One, Two, Three and Four.* These are essential viewing for anyone wanting to understand the importance of the foundations for learning.

9m Nutrition and Biochemistry

Dealing With Gut Problems & Food Intolerance Anywhere In The World

By Dr. Marilyn Dyson

Getting the body functioning optimally is the first basic step to increase performance and improve the effectiveness of therapies. So I always start with this. Once the dietary, nutritional, biochemical and health problems are being addressed, I start the motor programs, auditory stimulation therapies, visual training, etc, depending on the individual's needs. This seems to me an obvious approach: when the "hardware" (ie the body & biochemistry) is working efficiently, then the "software" (the programs to do various tasks) will be able to function more effectively. See chapter 4.

To achieve optimum function, I take the following steps:

1 Start with a good basic diet
2 Check for allergies and intolerances
3 Check for chemical intolerances
4 Check for the need for supplements
5 Check for the need to repair the gut
6 Look at inherited biological imbalances
7 Investigate other medical issues
8 Extra specific treatments for Autism and Asperger's Syndrome

A. ADHD, Learning Difficulties, Behaviour Problems and Allergy / Intolerance based Medical Problems

1. Start with a Good Basic Diet

Recent Australian research showed that more than 50% of Australians are not eating a balanced good diet. Only 30% are getting enough vegetables each day. The figures for deficiencies of basic nutrients like iron, iodine, folic acid and essential fatty acids are alarmingly high in the general Australian population. Also, most children are not drinking enough water.

These deficiencies in diet cause even greater problems for children with neuro developmental delays, as they need the nutrients to improve the function of their already compromised neurological systems.

They, as well as all children, will benefit from lots of water, fresh food and basic home cooking. For example, they have been shown to perform better with extra protein in their diet. For many of these children, more than 3 meals a day are necessary to maintain performance and good behaviour. So instead of carbohydrate snacks, give them mini meals (especially when they come home from school tired and cranky).

Daily Diet Recommendations

- 6 - 8 cups of liquid (mainly water with only a little juice, if any)

- 2 - 4 Fruits

- 5 - 8 Vegetables

- 1 Fish meal weekly (make sure it's low in mercury i.e.not large fish at the end of the food chain)

- Nuts, Seeds and Whole Grains

- Protein, protein, protein for breakfast, lunch and tea

- Complex Carbohydrates (i.e. low sugar, cakes, biscuits and white bread)

- No artificial additives (e.g. colouring, flavourings, preservatives etc.)

- Lots of variety

- Frequent Meals (up to 8 a day)

- A good breakfast every day

What about fussy eaters?

There are some children who are so fussy and rigid in their diets that it would be impossible to follow these recommendations. These children usually have either Autism Spectrum Disorders or food intolerances. They need to start with supplements and healing of the gut, followed by the removal of the foods to which they are intolerant. While this is happening, one should try to do as much as is possible of the diet above. After a few months, gradually and slowly, the range of foods that they will eat expands and the above recommendations become possible. For further helping ASD children, see the special section below.

2. Check for Food Allergies and Intolerances

It has been shown that children with neuro-developmental delays have an increased rate of allergies, ear infections, glue ear and other problems associated with atopy (ie allergy and intolerance).

A child with allergies or intolerances may start life with

- colic

- diarrhoea or

- constipation.

These may then settle (with or without dietary intervention) and then, over time, other medical conditions can develop. These may include

- eczema

- asthma

- irregular bowels

- respiratory and ear infections

- glue ear

- tonsillitis and/or

- rhinitis (with a runny itchy nose, sneeze, post nasal drip and cough).

These may continue or resolve, with the development of lethargy and/or poor concentration. This sequence of illnesses is all due to food allergy/intolerance.

It is important to understand that allergy and intolerance can present in a similar way. They can both cause the symptoms listed above. These children will often have signs that suggest underlying food problems, for example

- dark rings around their eyes (allergic shiners)

- puffy swelling under their eyes

- bumpy skin (nutmeg grater)

- white spots on their nails (because of low zinc levels) and

- smooth/cracks on their tongues (from a range of nutrients that are low)

- Red Ears or Cheeks

- Large Posterior Cervical Lymph Nodes

- Pot Belly

- "Adenoid" Face

- Mouth Breathing.

A GP, allergy specialist or immunologist will be able to diagnose and treat allergies. However, not many of these doctors understand the role, diagnosis or adequate treatment of intolerances. Many will test for allergies and then imply that, because the tests are negative, food is not part of the problem. This usually results in intolerances being ignored and the medical/behavioural problems continuing untreated.

When allergies and intolerances are looked for and treated, there are improvements in general health, behaviour, performance and learning. In addition, any therapies done for learning delays will be more effective. To check whether your child needs help for these types of problems, see *Help Your Child to Learn*, pages 63/64.

A person's history will often indicate when allergy is present, since allergic reactions tend to be immediate and obvious. However, lack of immediate, specific reactions to foods does not exclude the possibility of allergies.

Allergy is Immunoglobulin E mediated, and is usually associated with a high blood level of IgE. There are blood tests and skin prick tests to identify which food and/or inhaled allergens are problematic. These tests are very accurate in identifying an allergen if the result is positive. They are about 85% accurate if the result is negative.

Intolerances

With intolerances, there is often no history that indicates specific foods, because reactions can be delayed by up to 48 hours.

Intolerance is mediated by Immunoglobulin G. There are some blood tests to identify which foods are causing intolerances. However, mainstream medicine only uses the elimination diet to identify food intolerances.

The elimination diet removes all but a basic few foods that rarely cause intolerances. (It is no good taking out one food at a time, as it is rare that only one food is the problem. Thus, even though the one food that has been removed could be a problem, the other foods to which one is intolerant can still cause symptoms that mask any improvements.) Then, once there is improvement on the diet, one food at a time is reintroduced. If it causes symptoms, it needs to be taken out of the diet again until the person improves again.

This whole process of removal and reintroduction needs to be done a total of 3 times to be sure that this is an offending food (all the time keeping to the elimination diet 100%). If a food is not a problem, then it can be put back into the diet. Then this new diet is done for a few weeks before the next food is introduced. Needless to say this is a long and difficult process, especially for children and even more so for children who are fussy, rigid eaters or who have behaviour problems.

There is an easier and equally effective way to identify intolerances. There are a range of tests that some doctors and nutritionists use. The IgG food test and the cytotoxic food test are used the most. While they are not 100% accurate, they can be very helpful in identifying the main problem foods to be removed. I have found at least an 85% accuracy with these two tests – i.e. there has been improvement in the person's symptoms when the positive foods are removed from the diet for over 85% of patients.

Using these tests to identify the foods to be eliminated means that the subsequent diet is much easier to do. This greatly improves cooperation. There is no need to reintroduce and take out the foods repeatedly. (The children will cheat on the diet from time to time and this usually confirms to them and their parents the importance of remaining off that food!) When using this approach there is at least the same level of improvement as when doing the elimination diet as recommended by mainstream medicine.

For anyone on a diet for food allergies and/or intolerances, I recommend seeing a doctor, dietitian or nutritionist to ensure that your diet is adequate nutritionally. They can also recommend a range of nutrients and herbs that promote improved gut function and treat specific needs.

Treatment of Allergies and Intolerances

Both are treated in basically the same way :

- Identify

- Eliminate

• Heal the gut

• Add supplements

• Desensitisation (usually only done for severe allergies*)

• Re-introduction of some or all of the intolerant (& occasionally allergic) foods

*New methods for desensitisation for intolerant foods are currently being used, with variable results.

Coeliac Disease

It is essential to visit the doctor before starting any diet that has the potential to remove wheat. This is to clarify whether coeliac disease is present or not. (Once wheat is removed from the diet, the diagnosis of coeliac disease is virtually impossible without reintroducing wheat for a few months. Most people who have improved on a wheat free diet are very reluctant to reintroduce it for this period.)

It is important to test for coeliac disease because, if it is present, a 100% gluten free diet for the rest of life is essential. This is not only to improve one's health. It is essential to reduce the high risk of the range of cancers that are associated with coeliac disease.

In contrast, intolerances and allergies may, with treatment, improve to the degree where small, or even large, amounts of wheat can be eaten without any problems.

3. Check for Chemical Intolerances

Chemicals can cause a range of behavioural and medical problems. Children can become hyperactive, loud, impulsive and uncontrollable. Their ability to listen to and process what is being said to them can be markedly reduced. Some may develop medical problems, for example asthma and tummy aches. These reactions may occur within minutes of eating them, or may be delayed for a day or two.

Identification of chemical intolerances is similar to identification of food intolerances.

Added Chemicals

I recommend that everyone avoid chemicals that are added to food as much as possible. This includes the pesticides and herbicides that may be present in non-organic food. Reading the labels of some of our basic foods (e.g. bread) can be quite revealing as to the number and types of added chemicals we are consuming without realising it!

There is no doubt that some people are intolerant to specific food additives. These can be identified by the above tests or by the elimination diet. Avoiding such additives is initially useful for these people. These chemicals can usually be eaten without any noticeable reactions after treating food allergies/intolerances, the gut and the immune system (though of course I still recommend as few as possible be eaten).

Natural Chemicals

In the past, there has been an emphasis on reactions to naturally occurring chemicals such as salycilates, amines and MSG. Strict elimination diets (such as the diets of the Allergy Unit at Royal Prince Alfred Hospital and Sue Dengate) are commonly used to identify and eliminate these chemicals. This often results in an extremely limited, rigid diet with the exclusion of many fruit and vegetables.

However, although I too used to recommend starting with an elimination diet, I don't do so now. Instead I recommend first identifying and removing the intolerant/allergic foods. If there is no access to intolerance/allergy testing, I suggest eliminating milk products, wheat and any food(s) that the child seems to crave or eat in large amounts.

The next step is to heal the gut and add specific supplements. After this, I usually find that I rarely need to do the elimination diet for the removal of natural chemicals. The children are no longer reactive to these natural chemicals, and their behaviour and other symptoms have settled down.

4. Check for the need for Supplements

Supplements may be required for a range of reasons.

Restricted Diet

In **fussy eaters**, the range and the amount of essential minerals, vitamins, amino acids (from protein) and fatty acids eaten can be low.

Alternatively, when on **a diet that restricts certain foods**, the intake of certain specific nutrients can be reduced below the daily needed amount. For example, if a person is allergic or intolerant to milk and it has been removed from the diet, an adequate intake of calcium for one's age must be maintained. If this is not possible with food intake, a good calcium supplement (that also has magnesium) should be given.

In both instances, addition of the appropriate nutrients is beneficial.

Result of gut problems

When there has been a problem with **food intolerance/allergy or coeliac disease**, there can be gut damage as the result of eating these foods for many years. The lining of the gut can swell and became very inefficient in absorbing all the nutrients. The net result is reduction of essential nutrients. In addition, there can be micro haemorrhage into the gut that causes low iron levels.

It is useful to add multi-vitamins and minerals, as well as any nutrients that are specifically low.

To help heal the gut, add supplements like glutamine, glucosamine, aloe vera, pectin, slippery elm, fructo oligo saccharides, psyllium, vitamins A, C and E, zinc, selenium, carotenoids, folic acid, bioflavinoids and essential fatty acids.

Genetics

Research has shown that **Omega 3 Essential Fatty Acids (EFAs)** can be low in a high percentage of children with Learning Delays/Dyslexia, Motor and coordination delays/Dyspraxia and/or AD(H)D. It also has been shown that the addition of Omega 3 EFAs in the form of fish oils improves their symptoms and performance. A useful sign that suggests low omega 3 EFAs is the presence of cracks across the middle of the tongue.

Omega 6 levels can also be low in certain families. This results in dry skin that is more susceptible to eczema and dermatitis.

Research is also showing a number of **inherited biochemical problems** in people with ADHD, behaviour problems, ASD, anxiety, depression, bipolar disorder and schizophrenia. They can have low zinc levels (which is necessary for the formation of neurotransmitters in the brain). Some can also benefit from methionine or folic acid, which again improves neurotransmitter formation. However, **specific tests must be done** to ascertain which supplements are needed for each individual. (See the section on the Pfeiffer protocol for more details.)

To treat specific problems

Some supplements can have positive effects in their own right.

For example, **gingko** improves the blood flow and when this happens in the brain, brain function is improved. It has also been shown to increase the rate or formation of new dendrites (connections between nerves).

Prebiotics (eg Fructo Oligo Saccharide and Arabinase) and **Probiotics** (good bacteria) can also improve gut function by replacing lost beneficial bacteria. (It is important to note that they do NOT kill yeast/fungal infections.)

Sachromydes Boulardii can be used to kill fungal (especially candida) infections, and to allow the other good bacteria to grow.

Children with food intolerances (and often their siblings and even parents) may have white marks on their nails. This is a sign of **low zinc**. Zinc is important for good function of the skin, immune system, bones, gut enzymes and making of neurotransmitters. Low levels of zinc also can cause hypersensitivities to touch, taste, smell, light and sound. These people do better on zinc supplements. It is now possible to test plasma zinc levels to determine how much zinc is needed.

There are many other nutrients, herbs and supplements that can be beneficial, depending on the specific problems for each individual. I advise seeing an ACNEM Australian College of Nutrition and Environmental Medicine) trained doctor, naturopath or nutritionist who is trained in these areas.

5. Look at Inherited Biochemical Imbalances (Pfeiffer approach)

Karl Pfeiffer was a biochemistry researcher. He, along with other researchers, found that there was a range of certain biochemical problems associated with neuro developmental and psychiatric problems. These include people with ADHD, ASD, depression, anxiety, schizophrenia, behavioural disorders and anger/rage problems. Each of these medical diagnoses had a different combination/degree of biochemical problems.

He and others then developed protocols for treating each biochemical imbalance by adding specific supplements. The main imbalances are

• Low Zinc

- Copper/Zinc Imbalance

- Methylation problems

- Low Metallothionein production

- High Pyrrole levels

- Low Essential Fatty acids

- Heavy metals

The Pfeiffer website www.hirptc.org gives detailed information about these imbalances.

6. Other things that may need checking

When a patient comes to see me, the other things I would look for might include

- Constipation/faecal loading

This is especially so in ASD. Often there is a history of irregular and/or hard stools. However there can also be regular normal stools and even diarrhoea while the colon is loaded with stool.

- Infections in the gut

These can be foreign infections (like giardia, amoebae or Helicobacter pylorus), or the wrong types of bacteria (like beta Haemolytic Streptococcus).

- Gut dysbiosis

This is an imbalance of normal bacteria in the gut, often the result of antibiotics and other medicines. This is especially so in ASD, Chronic Fatigue Syndrome and Irritable Bowel Syndrome.

- Candida infection (thrush)

- Poor gut mucosa function (leaky gut)

- Low stomach acid

- Low digestive enzymes

- Other general infections (eg mycoplasma, streptococcus)

- Heavy metal levels

Not everyone has all, or even any, of these, but I check for them if the history and examination suggest they may be present.

B. Extra Treatments for Autism and Asperger's Syndrome (ASD)

People with Autism Spectrum Disorders (ASD) can often have all of the above problems. So I will always check for them and do the above treatments as appropriate. However, for people with ASD I usually start with a trial of the Gluten Free Casein Free (GFCF) diet. Another diet often helpful in ASD is the Specific Carbohydrate (SC) diet. See the web sites below for more detailed information on both these diets.

Gluten Free Casein Free (GFCF) diet

As one of the first things to do in ASD, I usually suggest all people with ASD trial a GFCF diet for 3-6 months. This is because in ASD there is a more than 50% probability of an enzyme deficiency in the gut (the DPPIV enzyme). At the moment there is no reliable test available to determine whether there is a DPPIV enzyme deficiency or not.

The lack of this enzyme leads to only partial digestion of gluten (the protein in many grains) and casein (**the protein in all animal milks**). As a result larger molecules of amino acid chains are formed (called gluto-morphs and caseo-morphs). These are then absorbed and travel to the brain. As they are a similar shape to certain neuro transmitters, they can occupy and block the neuro transmitter sites in

233

the neurones, thus causing reduced function in the brain.

It is usually easiest to do the GFCF diet in two steps - first remove the milk and milk products and then the gluten containing grains. Gluten is in wheat, barley, oats, rye spelt and a few other less common grains. I usually suggest that the person join the Coeliac Association as they are experts in removing gluten from the diet and, as they recognise the need for some ASD people to exclude gluten, they are very supportive.

If there is a DPPIV deficiency, the GFCF diet brings a significant step in improvement in many of the autistic symptoms. (Addition of the DPPIV enzyme can also help. It improves the digestion of gluten and casein by about 80%.)

Fussy, rigid eaters

The majority of ASD people are fussy about what they eat, with some being very rigid and only eating a very few foods. Usually wheat and milk are the main foods in the diets of these people. This means that trying to do any diet, let alone the GFCF diet, can seem almost impossible. However it can be done.

Sometimes it is possible to gradually remove casein products first. This can bring a step of overall improvement that then allows for subsequent removal of gluten containing foods.

Sometimes putting in the DPPIV enzyme along with other digestive enzymes and supplements can be enough to allow some improvement of the ASD symptoms and then the addition of other foods. Then a gradual reduction of casein and gluten foods is possible.

Sometimes there are other diet and gut problems and when these are treated, the removal of gluten and casein is possible. This is especially the case with the addition of supplements. For example, low zinc levels are very common in ASD and lead to hypersensitivity of smell, taste and touch (texture). These hypersensitivities can be major contributors to the fussy rigid diet. Thus, after the addition of zinc (usually using the

Pfeiffer approach that includes metallothionein promotion to improve the transport of zinc around the body), these hypersensitivities are reduced and there is a greater willingness to comply with increased dietary range and dietary change.

The involvement of a doctor, nutritionist or naturopath who has experience in the GFCF and SC diets is usually advised and can make the difference for success.

To sum up for ASD

Look for a doctor trained to do these protocols (eg a doctor trained by ACNEM - Australian College of Nutrition and Environmental Medicine, or a similar nutritional course). Get this doctor to go through these things with you. For the Pfeiffer protocol you will need a Pfeiffer trained doctor, so check their web site for the closest one for you.

The combination of the dietary approach plus the appropriate protocols as above is producing excellent results, which can then be foundational for further behavioral and neuro-developmental therapies specific to each individual's needs.

Medical Symptoms Associated with Allergy and Sensitivity

SKIN PROBLEMS

Eczema/ Dermatitis   Dry patches
Nutmeg grater skin   Itchy Skin

GASTRO-INTESTINAL PROBLEMS

Colic   Tummy pains or wind
Unusual bowel patterns   Constipation
White Spots on Nails   Diarrhoea
Irregularity   Bloating
Picky Eaters

EAR, NOSE & THROAT PROBLEMS

Mouth ulcers/itchiness   Bad breath
Glue Ear   Ear aches/Infection
Sinusitis   Persistent runny nose
Snoring   Mouth breathing
Rhinitis/Blood Noses   Bronchitis
Tonsillitis   Sneezing
Hay fever   Asthma

CENTRAL NERVOUS SYSTEM PROBLEMS

Poor memory   Irritability and/or aggression
Headaches   Inability to sit still
Inability to go to sleep   Bed wetting
Rocking cot/self   Head banging
Teeth grinding (Bruxism)   Night terrors or nightmares

Fluctuations in symptoms   Poor concentration
- day to day   - on all tasks
- hour to hour   - on disliked tasks only

VASCULAR PROBLEMS

Dizziness	Faintness
Pallor / coldness	Flushing

METABOLIC PROBLEMS

Excess activity	Known food allergies
Excess lethargy	Irritability relieved by food
Fluctuation between activity and lethargy	Craving for sweet things, salt, fluids, chocolate & other foods

FAMILY HISTORY

Any of the above issues identifiable in immediate family

White Spots on Nails	Dry Hair
Dry Skin	Nutmeg Skin
Eczema	Eye Shadows/Bags (Allergic Shiners)
Red Ears/Cheeks	Pot Belly
Mouth Breathing	'Adenoid Face'

Large Posterior Cervical Lymph Nodes
Furry/Smooth/Cracked/White Tongue

9n The Green Shed Girls Learn About Social Interaction

by Julia Dive

After working one-on-one with a variety of primary school students and knowing some of them personally, I perceived a need these children had which was not academic and was not being addressed by any remedial program.

The playground can be a very lonely and brutal place. Children who have difficulty following the pace in the classroom also have difficulty following the changing rules of the game. Understanding and executing some of the finer social skills which allow most other children to move in and out of games and situations, is very challenging and sometimes seems 'just not worth it'. The other area I wanted to explore, which is a little difficult one-to-one, was dance.

I suggested to the mothers of four of my past students that we get a small group of girls in years 4 and 5 together. The girls were all keen. So with the help of my friend and my 17 year old daughter we ran activities once a week for one and a half hours.

The first hour involved rotating bases every 15 minutes.

1. Rocking, rolling, crawling, flip-flopping.

2. Trampoline – Lefroy Sequences

3. Ladder sequences, mini tramp and balance beam

4. Other activity which varied weekly: sometimes a table activity e.g. sorting, and sometimes a moving activity e.g. skipping.

The other half an hour was spent talking about social interaction and doing a dance or rhythm activity.

Some other equipment we used included:

Copper rods: balancing on arms and heads, throwing and catching hand to hand.

Beanbags: balancing, throwing, catching, juggling.

Buttons: sorting, counting, deciphering codes.

Tub of water for soaking feet: warm water with lavender oil for calming, bubbles for interest and marbles to be dropped in and out with toes.

Sand tray: for calming (just running fingers through), hiding things, forming letters, and using small toys for social scenarios.

Big Gym ball: rolling over, under and also exercises.

Rockerboard: balance, combined with bean bags and balls.

Scooter board: upper body strength development.

Coloured blocks: sequencing and memory.

Poster with set pattern, which we followed with various combinations of hands/feet/eyes.

I used lots of ideas straight out of Barbara's books. I also incorporated some ideas from *Take Time* by Mary Nash-Wortham and Jean Hunt, The Robinswood Press.

I had spoken to our Support Teacher for Behaviour about some of the problems these children faced and she warned me, quite rightly, that the battle would be with the little voice inside their head which constantly confirmed their low self esteem. So armed with some books on the subject we plunged in.

Each week we took a different topic and the girls brainstormed different ideas and shared their experiences. We talked about how some situations made us feel and how the girls coped with them. Naturally, there was a lot of support from within the group as they had many experiences in common. Some of the topics we covered were: Positive tracking; Receiving and giving compliments; Do's and don'ts of being a good loser; Do's and don'ts of being a good winner; Speaking in front of an audience; Ignoring someone who

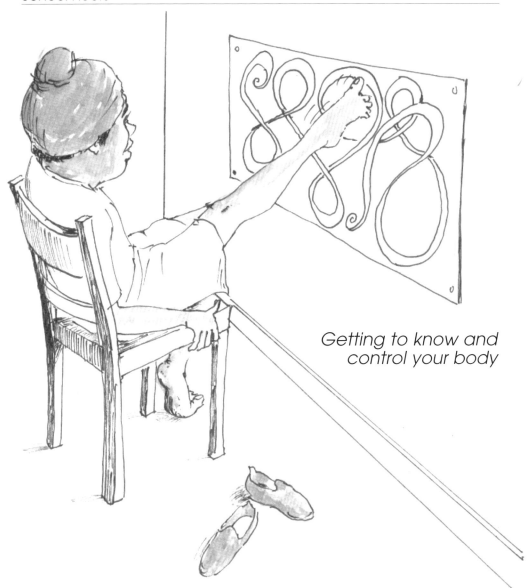

*Getting to know and
control your body*

is giving you a hard time; Telling someone to stop annoying you;
Listening and asking good questions. Each week the girls pasted a
short summary of the topic into their books in case they ever wanted
to brush up on some of their new skills.

Then more fun stuff – dancing. We started with a few simple bush
dances. Half of us had yellow pegs and half of us had white (no boy/girl
issues). So to good stirring music we did lots of movement involving
right, left, clockwise, anticlockwise, in, out, up, down, fast, slow. We
made up our own dance. We even managed to weave our way around the
circle in a chain. No mean feat but heaps of laughing and trying again.

Sometimes we clapped rhythm songs. Sometimes we worked in a circle with bean bags passing them in time to nursery rhymes. We also got a big rope and spent some time running in and out and skipping rhymes. We were even brave enough to try two big ropes at once. Just turning those in rhythm was hard enough let alone jumping them!! We had lots of fun and the girls were enthusiastic to develop their skills.

In order for them to put pen to paper through the week we had little open ended exercises which could take a page, a paragraph, a sentence, or even a picture. It gave them a chance to think about themselves and wasn't too demanding. Each week a different girl got to randomly choose a topic strip. (This was four lots of the same instruction stapled together.) She then gave everyone one each which they immediately glued into their books. That was their homework for the week. Topics included: How are you feeling today? Why? Draw it; Write a memory beginning 'I remember'; List five of your favourite things. Draw them; Describe something beautiful you saw yesterday. Draw it; What's the best thing that has happened this week? Given that each student was working off the same instruction the results varied widely but they were all happy to share the results each week.

I was hopeful, initially, that the program would run for six weeks. It was so successful we ended up running for twelve weeks and eventually had to stop because it was getting too cold and the days too short.

On the last day we had a party and a graduation ceremony. The girls all happened to have funny hats or wigs on. After they individually received their certificate and handshake we had a round of applause and then totally spontaneously they all threw their hats in the air. As a group they obviously felt very clever indeed! Yet again a reminder – don't underestimate their imagination!

9o Drumming

Integrating the Brain in a Fun Way

I'd like to introduce to you my drumming Teacher, Mike Almond, whose beginners' class in Afro/Latin rhythm and percussion I have just recently joined. I've always loved listening to drums and this was to be my special treat for 2006. Apart from that I also hoped that drumming with my hands would increase their strength and flexibility.

For those of us who don't own a drum, Mike has made a variety of Afro/Cuban drums with beautiful soft, tight hide covers which we can borrow. He also has bigger drums with drumsticks, cowbells, shakers and a band with bells for his right tapping foot.

Mike started the class by asking us each to introduce ourselves – but only using the drum. "How do you do that?" We 'newies' wondered. Fortunately Mike introduced himself first with a few taps and a smile.

*He then proceeded to teach us how to hit our drums in different places for different sounds. We were divided into groups to learn our own rhythm and then he gradually combined the groups so that we were all playing together and it sounded terrific. One or two of the more experienced students were led to come in with a 'solo' and I finished the morning feeling I had experienced a thrilling glimpse of what it would be like to be a part of an orchestra. **What a wonderful fun way to become integrated, to stimulate hands for handwriting and to be a part of a vibrant group of your peers.***

I asked Mike if he would be willing to share this with you, which he has generously done below, and you can use it if it sparks your imagination. It would follow on nicely after your students had done the movement sequence and their integration had already had a kick-start. If they got really interested it could then lead to more drumming and you, or someone who is a keen drummer in your community, could take the group further using the Internet for guidance. E.g. http://home.wandoo.nl/paul.nos/.

You could also just use bits of it as a 'break' for your class to help them relax and refocus. For example the class could march or sway and clap in 4/4 time while they said the alphabet and the special student of the day can hit the bell (tin cup) on the first pulse of every phrase.(see practical session below for explanation of 'pulse' and 'phrase')

*You might also have a 'jam session' with each student playing his or her instrument in 4/4 time with his or her own rhythm. The 'conductor' starts the first student off and then, when they are comfortable and focussed, another student is lead in to play his or her own rhythm at the same time. When this seems to be going well a third student starts and then a fourth etc. As a confidence booster, students could do this 'jamming' in pairs or small groups to help them to be able to maintain their own rhythm. These are just suggestions that keep popping into my head on Saturday mornings because it is such fun in the **controlled and accepting atmosphere** that Mike provides. You may not have the same reaction to it but possibly you might pass on this whole drumming thing to someone you know who could have fun with it.*

The promise of drumming in the future could also be a good 'bribe' or reward to help get older students on to the floor to do the movement sequences. – Barbara Pheloung

Your Journey in Musical Time – Mike Almond

In order to experience rhythms created by others, and enjoy making our own rhythms, we must first have a basic understanding of musical time and rhythmic notation.

The Concept of 'Four-Four' Time (notated as 4/4)

Pulse

For our purposes, **4/4 time** means four beats to a *bar* (or **measure**), and four *bars* to a *phrase*, which makes 16 notes in total. Each note has an individual name, so we can identify them, talk about them, and play them. Consider the following chart:

I've Got Rhythm

Pic 1.1: Basic 4/4 Time

Time	1				2				3				4			

Measure

The chart has a label at the beginning of the row called **Time**, then 16 boxes which each represents a musical beat. A nice feature of this system is that you can introduce it in very broad terms initially, and then refine the detail and the distinctions as the group progresses.

The Downbeat or *Pulse*

Okay, the first thing to do is to have your group **be together in time**. Have them chant what is known as the *pulse*: Say 'one, two, three, four' and repeat.

Now we add some context. Have them clap the *pulse* at the **One** as they loop the pattern.

If they are able, have the group stand, and step from side to side as they count. The more extroverted (or musically empowered) may well swing their hips whilst staying in time: You can make an early note as to potential dancers within the group!

At this point, you could substitute the counting, by having the group chant one of their favourite popular songs, whilst clapping the **One** *pulse*. Queen's *We will rock you,* is a good example, where you would clap on the words **we** and **rock**.

If you want to get even more adventurous, have the group step, clap (remember just the **One** *pulse* for the clap) and sing a song that does not start on the **One**, such as Robbie Williams' *Angel* where the first 'one' beat falls halfway through the word, wait '…I sit and wait …'

If they are getting into it, have them take it in turns to volunteer songs. After the group finishes, get them to applaud each other for their fine efforts.

Up-Beats

Okay, next step. We need to demonstrate and master the *up* beats that fall in between the numbers, so we double the notes learnt, from 4 up to 8.

Refer to the numbered notes as the main *down* beats, whilst the between notes are the *up* beats. This can be perfectly demonstrated if your group can stand-step. As they put down alternate R-L-R-L feet, count 1-2-3-4. The raised foot will be on the **'in-between'** note. For example, having played the **one** beat by putting your right foot down, in order to put your left foot down on the **two** beat, it will have to be up in the air for the **one and** (1&) up-beat. Try it!

Say 'one and two and three and four and'.

Step as you chant.

Remember to continue clapping the main **one beat** so you have a reference for the beginning of the rhythmic phrase.

Pic 1.2: 4/4 Time with main downbeats and upbeats shown

Additional Exercises to Master the 'and' beats in order to integrate all 8 notes

Exercise 1

Have the group clap the 1-2-3-4 as they chant the number. Then chant 1&2&3&4&.

When they are comfortable with that, have them emphasise the **'and'** beat, which will take place when their hands are furthest apart. See if you can get them stepping the R-L-R-L sequence at the same time. Now, once this is working well, the final step (if the group can sit or stand in a circle).

Whilst they are seated, make sure that they can reach and comfortably touch the flat of each others' hands.

Okay, when they do the **'and'** beat, get them to clap hands with the people either side of them. ie: a person will clap their right hands with the left hand of the person sitting to their right.

A variation of this is to get them to 'air clap' (or simply not clap) the 1-2-3-4 and just clap the 'ands' with their fellow musicians.

Exercise 2

Have the group move about an open space, counting 1-2-3-4 as they step R-L-R-L. They should be moving around and pacing in time together. Then ask the group to clap the 'and' beats as they walk around.

Hey, its okay if everyone falls in a heap laughing!!

If you think about it, you could probably think up all sorts of exercises to have your group enjoy learning their new rhythm skills... and we have only just scratched the surface!

Try to incorporate the notation chart into your rhythm workshops, so they start to become familiar with the matrix right from the start, and in its most simple form.

Above all, make sure they are comfortable and 'with you' at each level before you proceed further.

Our Rhythm: Beginners Start Here

Assuming you have mastered the rhythmic concepts, I think we are ready to create a rhythm... let's get playing!

First step is to choose our 'instrument': this can be a drum, a body, desk, bin, cardboard box... in fact anything that you can tap your hands on without hurting them (or the surface you are connecting with!)

For our rudimentary rhythm, we are going to get to know and use two basic percussive sounds:

The Bass or low-pitch sound

This is known as the **Bass** sound on a hand-drum: It is made by striking the middle of the drum with the flat of your hand. The principle is the same whatever you decide to use as your 'drum'. First practice using your voice: As you clap the pulse (the 1-2-3-4 beats), vocalise a deeeep guttural sound that emanates from your core in order to represent the low Bass sound on a drum, something like this:

Time	1		&		2		&		3		&		4		&	
Sing	Gun				Gun				Gun				Gun			

The Tone or high-pitch sound

Now we introduce the second of our two sounds, which is the high-pitch or the *Tone* sound. On a hand-drum it is made by striking the rim of your drum with just the length of your fingers (ie: not using the palm of the hand). This makes a higher sound, which we can vocalise as a *ga* or *ta* sound (voice it as high as possible to hear the distinction). Now we can vocalise the two sounds in the same musical space. The new sound is in **bold.** Practice:

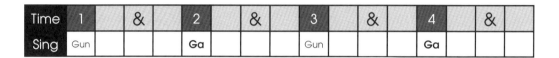

Time	1		&		2		&		3		&		4		&	
Sing	Gun				**Ga**				Gun				**Ga**			

Once you get used to singing the two pitches in time (remember to clap the pulse as you sing) it is time to move back to your drum/bin/box etc. Remember to play the lower *gun* sound in the middle of the instrument and the higher *ga* on the rim or edge of your instrument.

When playing your instrument: at this stage just use whatever hand combinations (R/L) you are comfortable with.

Once you are okay with this, we can start to make the rhythm more interesting. Try this:

Rhythm #1: Sung

Time	1		&		2		&		3		&		4		&	
Sing	Gun				**Ga**				Gun		Gun		**Ga**			

If we are counting, we would say 'one, two, three-and-four'. It's important you can sing or vocalise this whilst you (or a friend) claps the pulse. Again, when you are comfortable with the rhythm, transfer the sound from your voice to your hands and play your instrument! Here is how we would notate for a drum:

Rhythm #1: Played on your instrument

Time	1		&		2		&		3		&		4		&	
Play	B				T				B		B		T			

Remember B is the **Bass** or *Low Note* on your drum, and T is the **Tone** or *High Note* on your drum.

Last Steps...

Okay, this is where it gets really cool: we are going to create a 'polyrhythmic effect'. This simply means we are going to sing or play two different rhythms at the same time. When this in done in time, it creates the effect of a combined rhythm.

Rhythm #2: Sung

Time	1		&		2		&		3		&		4		&	
Sing	Ga		Ta		Ga		Ta									

Rhythm #2: Played on your instrument

Time	1		&		2		&		3		&		4		&	
Play	T		T		T		T									

Now play them both together:

Start by having a person (or group of people) clap the pulse. Then have your allocated **Rhythm #1 group** sing their part. When that is grooving, have your **Rhythm #2 group** add their part. Once you master this notion the possibilities are endless! Have fun!!

For more experienced performers...

The Next Step: The Infamous 3-2 Clave

Add this rhythm part to your performance once you have mastered it.

If you are ready to take the next big step, it's time to learn the most fundamental and popular of cowbell patterns; the **3-2 Clave.** It is known this way because it has a group of three notes, followed by a group of two. It is played across the globe, and forms the heartbeat for countless popular songs.

We learn the Clave by first clapping the **pulse**, then singing the part in a way that helps us to feel the syncopation of the rhythm:

Pic 2a: 3-2 Clave (Sung)

Time	1		&		2		&		3		&		4		&	
Sing	Ke	en	i	Ke	en	i	Ka				Cha		Cha			

Once we can sing the part, we move the **Time** from our hands, down to our feet. This frees our hands to take over from our voice. We pass the **Clave pattern** from voice to hands so we can now clap the Clave in time and keep a cool groove happening!

Once we are familiar with the rhythm, we can dispense with the singing part, and just annotate the rhythm as follows:

So, here comes something else that is new – the bell or tin cup.

Pic 2b: 3-2 Clave (played)

Time	1	e	&	a	2	e	&	a	3	e	&	a	4	e	&	a
Play	X			X			X				X		X			

If you can sing and play this whilst you tap the pulse with your feet (or have a friend clap the pulse), you will be hooked for life!

For more information on Mike and his teaching style, look at his web site, www.feelrhythm.com.au.

9p Movement and the Use of 3 dimensional Objects Helps Students to Understand Number Work More Easily

It might be helpful to discuss the three stages of learning and how our understanding of this can help us as we are endeavouring to help our children with mathematics homework.

The illustration on the next page shows the three stages.

Pre-school learning is done mainly through 3 dimensional objects and movement even though some experience of pencil and paper work often starts before school. At school, students are gradually given more and more 2 dimensional experience with the introduction of words and numbers on pieces of paper. This should only be encouraged, not pressured, because if a student is not ready for pencil and paper, 2 dimensional work it will put unnecessary pressure on them and slow down the learning process.

Movement and concrete objects to solidify Mathematics

The 3 stages of learning:

Concrete Thinking

2-Dimensional

Abstract Thinking

The same thing applies when learning concepts. This should never be rushed and it sometimes occurs in mathematics that a child is asked to do abstract thinking and memory work while they still need concrete or 3 dimensional learning material. This can even happen in High School and it makes for unnecessary failure. It is not a sign of stupidity if a student needs to rely on things like cuisenaire blocks or abacus calculators. It merely means that they should be allowed 3 dimensional aides to learning as long as they want them. When they don't need them they won't use them. If they don't have this facility in the classroom parents can at least provide concrete objects for use during homework.

Glossary

Acuity: Clarity of vision. The standard is 20/20, which means that at a distance of 20 feet (6 metres) the individual can see objects clearly.

Apgar score: A method of rapidly assessing the general state of a baby immediately after birth. A maximum of 2 points is given for each of the following signs—type of breathing, heart rate, colour, muscle tone and response to stimuli. Thus, an infant scoring 10 points at 60 minutes after delivery would be in optimum condition. When the score is low the test is repeated at intervals as a guide to progress.

Apraxia: The inability to plan motor movements of your own body.

Asperger's Syndrome: This is one of five neurobiological pervasive developmental disorders, and is characterised by normal intelligence and language development, but with deficiencies in social and communication skills.

Associative memory: The process of relating or connecting thoughts, concepts and remembering them.

Astigmatism: A condition in which the eyeball or lens are mis-shapened causing the eyes to be out of focus, the effect being a distortion.

Atopy: The genetic tendancy to develop the classic allergic diseases; i.e. atopic dermatitis, allergic rhinitis.

Auditory closure: The ability to recognise the meaning of spoken language when parts are missing.

Auditory discrimination: The learned ability to notice and understand differences in sounds. It is not concerned with actual hearing but interpreting what is heard.

Auditory figure-ground discrimination: The ability to hear what we want to hear in spite of background noise.

Auditory perception: The learned skill of acquiring meaning out of what is heard.

Auditory: Concerned with the sense of hearing.

Auditory-motor – Bilateral: Refers to the use of both sides of the body at the same time when listening.

Auditory-motor – Binocular: Refers to the use of both eyes together when listening.

Auditory-Motor: The ability to move the body in response to what is heard.

Auditory processing: The ability related to the ear to effectively register and then process what is heard so that the brain can interpret meaningfully the sounds that surround him for speech and its role in language (communicating with others), learning and literacy.

Bilateral integration: The integration of the two sides of the body and the two halves of the brain so that the body functions efficiently as one whole.

Bilateral: Can refer to the use of both sides of the body at the same time.

Bilateral Motor Integration: This is the working of the two sides of the body together in a way that one assists the other side's movement for a task.

Body awareness: A person's awareness and idea of his own body and its parts and how they function in space and in relationship to their own body.

Body concept: A learned awareness through language of the names of the various body parts.

Body image: The idea that a person has about his own body, e.g. fat, just right, too tall, beautiful, etc.

Body schema: The unconscious body awareness which develops through messages from the tactile, proprioceptive, kinaesthetic and vestibular systems.

Body Space: An always present, automatic sense of where one is during varied activities.

Brain biofeedback or neurofeedback: A device that helps those with Attention Deficit Disorder to control their attentional mechanisms. Electrodes on the head feed into a biofeedback machine enabling them to monitor their brain waves and adjust their behaviour accordingly.

Brain imaging techniques: These modern techniques allow us to not only get detailed pictures of the anatomy of the brain but also allow us to study the uptake of glucose while different tasks are done. This enables us to see how well each area of the brain is being used for each specific task.

Brain Integration (right and left sides): Where the skills or abilities of each side of the brain work interactively and not in competition or without each other. This is optimal for body and hand coordination, as well as reading, and maths and all mental and learning tasks. This should be accomplished by 7 or at the very latest 8 years of age.

Cerebral Palsy: A disorder in movement, posture and muscle tone caused by brain damage in a developing brain that is considered to remain throughout life.

Clinical assessment: Formal or informal testing 'in clinic' which tries to understand an individual child's best way of learning.

Closure: The ability to perceive something as a whole even if some parts are missing.

Cognitive learning: Learning that comes from using the thinking part of the brain, as in reflection, perception, comprehension and observation.

Context strategies (words): Methods of understanding the meaning of a new word from the language that surrounds the word.

Criterion-referenced testing: Testing of how a child does a certain thing in order to compare this with how he did it before.

Cross-pattern/contralateral movement: Movement that requires opposite arms and legs to move interactively together, e.g. when walking and crawling.

Developmental delay: A slow and usually uneven maturing in a child's neurological development across such areas as language, social, gross motor and hand skills.

Dexterity: A high level of coordination of the hands and fingers to undertake varied skills needed for daily play, self-care and learning.

Differentiation (in regard to the use of the body): The ability we have to hold one part still and use another part independently, e.g. when moving only one finger at a time or the pencil grip fingers working and the fourth and fifth fingers supporting them.

Diplopia: Double vision.

Directionality: An awareness of direction (left/right, up and down) which develops after we automatically know the left and right sides of our own body and a dominant hemisphere or lateralisation develops.

Distractibility: The inability to pay attention because of being too easily distracted, e.g. not being able to screen out distracting information and being able to hold attention on the relevant information.

Dominance: The tendency of one side of the body to be more developed than the other and to lead the other side, e.g. right-handedness.

Educational Kinesiology (EK): EK enhances our ability to learn by improving right and left brain coordination. It draws upon the knowledge of brain process, remedial educational techniques and some of the principles of oriental medicine.

Educational psychology: A science which involves the testing of a child's academic abilities. The sub-tests for the LD child often reveal specific strengths and weaknesses.

Esotropia: A condition where one eye turns inwards.

Evoked brain potentials: This measures how a particular part of the brain handles a stimulus, allowing us to see if there is delayed or dysfunctional processing.

Exotropia: A condition where one eye turns outwards.

Expressive language: The way we communicate to other people through language (talking, using signing or visual cues) and gesture.

Eye-hand co-ordination: The ability to use eyes and hands together well for fine and gross motor activities, e.g. for tracing and when ball catching.

Eye-teaming (convergence, divergence): The way the eyes work together as a team to look in close for reading and to look at the distance for copying from the board.

Feedback: A sensory process by which the individual monitors his own performance, consciously or unconsciously. For example, joints and muscles give the brain feedback as to the position of the limbs of the body.

Feldenkrais Method: A system of learning through body awareness and movement of more appropriate ways of holding posture, moving or doing an activity to suit the individual.

The 'fidgeter': A child that constantly and unconsciously handles and manipulates items, not necessarily in a constructive way.

Fine motor dexterity: The ability to control the small muscles of the body, primarily in the eyes and hands, necessary to successfully perform such fine motor tasks as handwriting as well as tongue movements for eating and speaking.

Finger-slide: A three-way process of learning to read: the child looks at the words, follows them across the page with one finger, and listens to the Teacher reading them.

Frequency: Sound reaches our ears in the form of sound waves which are variations in air pressure over time. Frequency is the rate at which air particles vibrate. A slow rate would be a low frequency sound, e.g. a cow 'mooing'; a high rate would be a high frequency sound, e.g. a violin.

Glue ear: This is a congestion of puss and mucus inside the tubes of the ear drum which impairs hearing. Children are more susceptible to this condition because their tubes are narrower and don't drain as easily. The liquid needs to drain away so that the ear drum can be filled with air through which sound waves can pass easily.

Gross motor: The movement of the larger muscles of the body which produce good total body movement, e.g. running.

Hertz: The unit of measure of frequencies. Young children can hear up to 20,000 hertz.

Homolateral /unilateral movement: Exercises where members of the same side of the body are used together. (e.g. left arm, left leg and head to the left).

Hyper-: refers to an increase, e.g hypertonia would be an increase in muscle tone or 'tight' muscles. It also describes a condition of any of the sensory systems which allows an excess of sensory stimulation to the brain.

Hyperkinetic behaviour: Excessive and uncontrolled movement.

Hyperopia (long-sightedness): Effort needs to be made to keep things clear at a reading distance.

Hypo-: refers to a decrease or lowering. e.g hypotonia would be a decrease in muscle tone or 'soft' muscles. It also describes a sluggish sensory system which doesn't allow enough of the sensory stimulation to reach the brain.

Hypoglycemia: Not enough sugar in the blood to meet a person's energy requirements.

Kinaesthesia: The conscious sense of movement and position of the body and its parts. The brain receives this information from the joints, tendons and muscles.

Laterality: The inner awareness of the left and the right sides of our own body and the ability to spontaneously choose the one needed for a task. It depends on one side of the brain 'taking charge' so that particular abilities or functions are not being led by both sides.

Leaky Gut: The lining of the gut can be damaged by infection, allergies/food intolerances and antibiotics. As a result you can have inefficient absorption of nutrients and when the larger molecules go across from the gut to the blood stream there are increasing health risks.

Midline: This is an imaginary line which divides a person's body in half. It acts like a wall in babies but it disappears at around three to four years through normal play and movement. When it persists after this time it interferes with the development of coordinated activity where the body has to act as a whole organism. It also slows down academic work when both sides of the brain should work easily together.

Midline Crossing: Eyes, arms, hands and legs should work with ease across the middle of the body which is particularly pertinent to hand and upper body coordination.

Minus lenses: Concave lenses which enable eyes to focus farther away.

Mnemonic devices: Methods of association of images, words or ideas to assist memory.

Moro reflex: This is a primitive reflex for the purpose of survival. When a baby feels threatened or startled he throws his head back, his arms forward, arches his spine and straightens his legs so he can get his lungs full of air to cry for help. This develops into the adult startle reflex at around six months.

Morpheme: A letter or group of letters which have meaning. It is either a part of a word or a whole word, e.g. be-long-ing.

Motor activity: The movement or response to sensory input. The nervous system can direct the action at an automatic (e.g. the response to touching a hot stove) or at a conscious level (e.g. lifting a box of groceries).

Motor planning: The planning required in the brain before the body is able to do a series of movement actions.

Motor: To do with body movement or posture.

The 'mouther': A child that constantly and unconsciously puts things in his mouth.

Myopia (short-sightedness): Difficulty in seeing things in the distance.

Near-to-far and far-to-near fixations: The ability of the eyes to refocus quickly, e.g. being able to refocus on a book on a desk after copying from a blackboard.

Neurological immaturities: A slowness seen in a child's natural development of inherent optimal functioning for the expectation for their age or stage of development. It is not brain damage, but can be treated in the same way.

Neurological organisation: This is the process by which a human being achieves his/her potential, subject to environmental forces, which is reliant on the nervous system developing in its inherent and orderly way.

Normed: A test is normed if it is able to compare a student's performance with others the same age or in the same grade.

Norm-referenced testing: Testing that shows how a pupil performs compared to others the same age or in the same grade.

Obstacle courses: In *Overcoming Learning Difficulties* we refer to structured activities which combine a number of areas of learning into a challenging fun activity at the level at which a child is able to perform them.

Ocular motor skill (eye-movement): A learned skill of using the eyes accurately and efficiently in the directions needed for reading, work in the classroom, etc.

PALD: Professional Association for Learning Difficulties. A Sydney based Inter-professional Association for Learning Difficulties which ran in Sydney, Australia from approximately 1970 to 2005, changing its name in that time to **PHLD (Professional Help for Learning Difficulties).**

Perception: The meaning that we make out of what we see, hear, smell, taste and/or feel.

Peripheral vision: The ability to see from the outer rim of the eyes to the sides while looking directly at something in front.

Perseveration: The act of repeating something over and over again.

Phonetic ability: Being able to work out a word by sounding out its letters, e.g. c–a–t = cat.

Pitch: A person's perception of frequency. e.g. low pitch for low frequency.

Plantar Reflex (foot): This is an early primitive reflex flexion or 'gripping' of the toes when contact is made to the pads of the soles of the feet which needs to integrate or disappear at around three months of age.

Plus lenses: Convex spectacles used mostly to make focusing on print easier, thus relieving the strain.

Position in space: Sufficient awareness of ourselves and the space around us to determine our position in relation to other objects. It also relates to the two-dimensional perceptual ability of position, e.g. the ability to differentiate between *b, d, g, p, q* etc.

Primitive reflexes: These are early wired-in movements that help the movement of all babies in the womb and their new movements after birth. When they are no longer needed they make way for postural reactions and 'automatic body control' that allows for purposeful movement.

Primitive Reflex Integration: The 'inherent program in the developing brain and body' by which the early primitive reflex patterns become less apparent to inactive and allows the next developmental movement to occur, i.e. the next stage of primitive reflex or a mature pattern of movement.

Proprioception: The internal information sent from the muscles, joints and tendons to the brain so that automatic adjustments can be made, e.g. to stand on one leg without falling over when kicking a ball.

Receptive language: The way we hear and understand what others communicate to us.

Retained Primitive Reflexes: These are reflexes that remain active after they are no longer needed and become a barrier to easy natural movement development, i.e. achieving the next milestone.

Retrieval: The process of recalling/retrieving information from memory.

Reversal: Seeing letters, numerals or words in reverse position, e.g. *b* for *d*, *E* for *3*, *was* for *saw*. It can also refer to writing and speaking.

SAMONAS Sound Therapy - (Spectrally Activated Music of Optimal Natural Structure): Uses very specialised CDs which are listened to through headphones. It is used to treat those with dyslexia, learning or behaviour problems, attention deficit disorder/ autism, developmental delays as well as adult hearing problems. It was developed by Ingo Steinbach who describes it as "micromassage of the muscles within the middle ear preparing the organism for further stimuli". This results in the stimulation of the total brain.

Sensory input: The information that comes to us from our senses-through hearing, seeing, smelling, tasting and feeling (from skin and movement).

Sensory Integration Therapy: Devised by Dr. A Jean Ayres. Used by qualified Occupational Therapists and Physiotherapists. Uses formal and informal assessments of the individual's level of maturity in body senses (touch, movement, balance, body/muscle), postural control for hand and body coordination and visual perception that is needed for play, social skills and emotional and learning development. It is individualised therapy using sensory based gross and fine motor interactive play.

Sensory motor integration: The maturity that occurs in the brain when the child undertakes much physical play activity which is developmentally appropriate, incorporating touch stimulation to the skin, movement and balance (vestibular) and strong muscle (proprioceptive) work. This stimulates lower brain processing which is involved in basic eye and postural control, body and spatial awareness, and processing which is important for learning and more abstract thinking.

Sensory Preparation: Stimulation of the skin and muscle sensors to assist the reactions of the muscles to do organised movements needed for specific tasks.

Sequencing skills: An awareness that there is an orderly arrangement in the nature of things and that there are causes and effects. This is one of the basics needed for timing and fluency in physical and mental skills.

Spatial awareness: The awareness of what is around you – the position and size of surrounding objects and their distance from you and each other. It is preceded by an accurate awareness of your own body.

Spatial relationships: An ability developed from spatial awareness— the accurate awareness of the relationship of objects and symbols to each other in the space around us, e.g. the position of letters and words in relation to each other on a piece of paper.

SPELD: The initials for the organisation called Specific Learning Difficulties Association. They are several voluntary associations operating independently in Australia and New Zealand. SPELD NSW was started by Yvonne Stewart in 1968 and now operates out of St. Ives, NSW, 7 Acron Rd.

Stereopsis: (Depth perception): The ability to judge relative distances of objects and see and move in three-dimensional space, e.g. when hitting a ball.

Strabismus: A condition in which one eye or both eyes are turned.

Syllabising: The dividing of words into syllables.

Tactile: Refers to the sense of touch on the skin. We get information from our skin about temperature, pain, pressure and what we are touching or what is touching us.

Tactility: The feelings of temperature, pain and pressure sent to the brain from the skin and vice versa.

The 'tigger': A child who is over-energetic, unconsciously moving, often bumping, pushing, and pulling items and people.

Timbre: A subjective description of the tone or resonance of the voice or instrument.

Toddler Kindy Gymbaroo: An organisation specializing in preparing children to be ready to learn through movement activities – both pre-school and school children. Branches all over Australia and in New Zealand. Started and directed by Margaret Sasse in Melbourne and linked originally with *ANSUA: A New Start for the Underachiever.* www.gymbaroo.com.au.

Tripod finger grip: Thumb, index and middle fingers work together for hand writing.

Unilateral movement: One side of the body moving together at a time.

Vestibular system: gives us our spatial orientation so we don't fall over. Helps to bring together messages from our eyes, its sensors in our ears and muscles give us a sense of balance. It is affected by the position of our heads in relation to the ground as well as by increasing or decreasing movement in all planes/directions.

Visual: To do with the sense of sight.

Visual accommodation: Focusing of the eyes.

Visual closure: The ability to recognise objects, letters and words when only part of them is seen.

Visual discrimination: The learned ability to notice and understand differences in what is seen. It is not to do with actual sight but with interpreting what is seen.

Visual figure-ground discrimination: The ability to visually distinguish something from its background.

Visual focus: The ability to accurately look at an object and keep it clear for a period of time. This is an important skill for reading to prevent tiredness.

Visual perception: The learned skill of making sense out of what you see.

Visual: To do with the sense of sight.

Visual processing: The ability of the visual system to effectively register and then process what is seen so that the brain can meaningfully interpret the environment, situation, objects, people and symbols around it. Needed for safety, interaction and guiding movements, and particularly later for 2D learning, reading and writing.

Visualisation: The ability to picture something in your mind. A most necessary skill for reading comprehension and social skills.

VMP: Variably Maladjusted Primitives Study Group. An inter-professional group, started in Sydney, Australia in 1994, networking around their common concern, Learning Difficulties.

Word finding: The ability with language to find the right word quickly for the topic at hand.

Bibliography

A.C.L.D. compiled by Mann, C. *My Child Can Learn*. A.C.L.D. NSW.

Academic Therapy; interdisciplinary journal. Academic Therapy Publications, Inc.

ACHPER and the Australian Trampoline Sports Union Inc. *Trampoline Sports, Aussie Sports Coaching Program*. Endorsed by the Australian Coaching Council as an approved level 0 Coaching Course Manual. ACHPER Publications, 128 Glen Osmond Rd., Parkside, SA 5063, 1988.

Arnheim, D. D. and Sinclair W. A. *The Clumsy Child; a program of motor therapy, 2nd Ed.* the C. V. Mosby Company, 1979.

Auckett, A. D. *Baby Massage*. Hill of Content Publishing Co., 1981.

Auditory Processing Disorder Seminar, 2004 Video/DVD. Adelaide: Women's and Children's Hospital Production.

Aukerman, R. C. *Approaches to Beginning Reading*. John Wiley and Sons Inc, 1971.

Auspeld Workshop Proceedings. Papers presented at the 1972 Auspeld-Anu Workshop on specific learning disabilities, 1972.

Australian Remedial Mathematics Education Association. *Success in Learning Mathematics (4 Vols.)*. Victoria, Australia: 1986.

Ayres, A. J. *Sensory Integration and the Child*. Western Psychological Services, 1979.

Banas, N. and Wills, I. H. *WISC-R Prescriptions: How to work creatively with individual learning styles*. Academic Therapy Publications, 1978.

Barnes, B. and Colquhoun, I. *The Hyperactive Child; What the Family Can Do*. Thorsons Publishers Ltd., 1984.

Behrmann, P. *Activities for Developing Visual Perception*. Academic

Therapy Publications, 1970.

Behrmann, P. and Millman, J. *Excel, and Excel II.* Educators Publishing Service, Inc., 1968.

Bell, N. *Visualising and Verbalising; for Language Comprehension and Thinking.* Academy of Reading Publications, 1986.

Berard, Guy. *Hearing Equals Behaviour.* Keats Publishing, 1993.

Bergland, R. *The Fabric of Mind.* Penguin Books, 1985.

Bever, S. *Building a Child's Self-Image; a guide for parents.* The Minnesota Association for Children and Adults with Learning Disabilities, 1982.

Bluestone, Judith. *The Churkendoose Anthology - True Stories of Triumph Over Neurological Dysfunction.* Handle Institute, 2002.

Bluestone, Judith. *The Fabric of Autism.* HANDLE Institute, 2004.

Boehme R. *Improving Upper Body Control: an Approach to Assessment and Treatment of Tonal Dysfunction* Therapy Skill Builders, a Division of Communication Skill Builders, Tucsan Arizona USA, 1988.

Braley, W.T., Konicki, G. and Leedy, C. *Daily Sensorimotor Activities. Educational Activities.* Freeport New York: 1985.

Brooks, M. M. and Engmann-Hartung. *Your Child's Speech and Language; guidelines for parents.* h and h enterprises, Inc., 1978.

Brutten, M., Richardson, S., and Margel, C. *Something's Wrong with My Child: A Parent's Book about Children with Learning Disabilities.* New York: Harcourt Brace Jovanovich, 1973.

Buist, Dr. R. *Food Intolerance.* Harper and Collins, 1993.

Bullus, J. and Coles, P. *Perceptual Motor Programs.* Victoria, Australia: PJ Developments, 1987.

Bush, W. J. and Giles, M. T. *Aids to Psycholinguistic Teaching,* 2nd

Ed. Charles Merrill Publishing Co., 1977.

Cairns, S. and Pieterse, M. with Treloar, R. and Cross, M. *T.E.L.L.*, 2nd Ed. Macquarie University, 1983.

Capon, J. J. *Perceptual Motor Development Series*, 5 vols. Pitman Learning, 1975.

Carter, A. E. *The Miracles of Rebound Exercise.* The National Institute of Reboundology and Health, Inc., 1979.

Chaney, C. M. and Kephart, N. C. *Motoric Aids to Perceptual Training.* Charles Merrill Publishing Co., 1968.

Clark, M. M. *Teaching Left-Handed Children.* Hodder and Stoughton, 1974.

Cloud, Dr. Henry and Townsend, Dr. John. *Boundaries, When to say Yes, When to say No.* Sydney, Australia: Strand Publishing, 2000.

Cohen, M. E. *Bets Wishs Doc.* Penguin Books Inc., 1975.

Craig, E. *PS You're not listening.* New American, 1972.

Crook, W .G. *You and Allergy.* Professional Books, 1980.

Crook, W. G. *Are you Bothered by Hypoglycemia?* Professional Books, 1977.

Crosby, R. M. *Reading and the Dyslexic Child.* Souvenir Press, 1968.

Cruickshank, W. M. Editor. *The Teacher of Brain-Injured Children; a discussion of the bases for competency.* Syracuse University Press, 1966.

Cutler-Stuart, M. *How to Write Essays, A Practical Guide for Students.* Hale and Iremonger, 1985.

Davis, A. *Let's Get Well.* Unwin Paperback, 1965.

Davis, Ronald D. *The Gift of Dyslexia*, rev. ed. Ability Workshop Press, 1994.

Delacato, C. H. *A New Start for the Child with Reading Problems.* New York: David McKay Co. Ltd., 1970.

Delacato, C. H. *The Diagnosis and Treatment of Speech and Reading Problems.* Springfield, Illinois, USA: Charles C. Thomas, 1963.

Delacato, C. H. *The Ultimate Stranger.* Doubleday and Co. Inc., 1974.

Dengate, Sue. *Fed Up.* Random House, Australia, 1998.

Diamond, M. and Hopson, J. *Magic Trees of the Mind.* Penguin, 1998.

Dobson, J. *Dare to Discipline.* Tyndale House Publishers, 1971.

Dobson, J. *Discipline while you can.* Eastbourne: Kingsway Publications, 1981.

Doman, G. *What to Do about Your Brain-Injured Child.* Jonathan Cape, 1974.

Doyle, J. *Practical Audiology for Speech and Language Therapists.* London: Whirr Publishers, 1998.

Duffy, G. and Sherman, G. *Systematic Reading Instruction,* 2nd ed. Harper and Row, 1977.

Eady, J. *Additive Alert.* Mullaloo, Western Australia: Additive Alert Pty Ltd., 2004.

Education Department of Western Australia. *The Fundamental movement skill assessment manual.* 151 Royal Street, East Perth, WA 6004: Education Department of Western Australia, 1997.

Ekwall, D. D. *Locating and Correcting Reading Difficulties.* Charles Merrill Publishing Company, 1970.

Elijah House Inc. www.elijahhouse.org

Ellis, J. and Whaite, A. *To Parents of Children with Special Needs.* Family and Children's Services Agency. *From Parents of Children with Special Needs.* A series of 7 pamphlets. Canberra: Shield Press 1987.

Feingold members throughout the United States. *The Feingold Handbook.* The Feingold Association of the United States, 1983.

Feldenkrais, M. *Awareness through Movement. Health exercises for personal growth.* Penguin Books, 1980.

Ferreri, C. and Wainwright, R. *Breakthrough for Dyslexia and Learning Disabilities.* Exposition Press of Florida, 1984.

Finnie, N. R. *Handling the Young Cerebral Palsied Child at Home,* 2nd Ed., London: William Heinemann Medical Books Ltd., 1974.

Flesch, R. *Why Johnny Can't Read.* Harper and Row, 1986.

Frostig, M. *Movement Education: theory and practice.* Chicago: Follett Educational Corporation, 1970.

Frostig, M., Horne, D. and Miller, A. *Pictures and Patterns; the developmental program in visual perception,* 4th Australasian Ed. Follett Publishing Company, 1975.

Fulwood, D. and Cronin, P. *Facing the Crowd. Managing other people's insensitivities to your disabled child.* Royal Victorian Institute for the Blind, 1986.

Furth, H. G. and Wachs, H. *Thinking Goes to School; Piaget's theory in practice.* Oxford University Press, 1975.

Garbourg, P. *The Secret of the Ring Muscles.* Ora International Grafix, 1997.

Getman, G. N. *How To Develop Your Child's Intelligence.* P.O. Box 636, White Plains, Md., 20695-0636, USA: Research Publications, 1962.

Gilbert, A. G. *Teaching the Three Rs through movement experiences.*

Bethesda, Maryland: Prentice-Hall Inc., 2002.

Gillham, W. E. C. *Teaching a Child to Read.*
Hodder and Stoughton, 1974.

Goddard, S. *Reflexes, Learning and Behaviour.*
Fernridge Press, 2002.

Goddard, Sally. *A Teacher's Window into the Child's Mind and papers from the Institute for Neuro-physiological psychology* (INPP) Director Peter Blythe. Eugene, Oregon, USA: Fernridge Press, 1996.

Gold, Svea J. *When Children Invite Child Abuse.*
Fernridge Press, 1986.

Golick, M. *A Parent's Guide to Learning Problems.*
Quebec Assoc. for Children with Learning Disabilities.

Golick, M. *Deal Me In.* Jeffrey Norton, 1981.

Goodacre, E. J. *Children and Learning to Read.*
Routledge and Kegan Paul, 1971.

Goodman, Y. M. and Burke, C. with Sherman, B. *Reading Strategies; Focus on Comprehension.*
Holt, Rinehart and Winston, 1980.

Grasselli, R. N. and Hegner, P A. *Playful Parenting. Games to help your infants and toddlers grow physically, mentally and emotionally.*
Perigee Books, 1981.

Green, C. *Toddler Taming.* Double Day, 1984.

Grounds, A. *The Hyperkinetic Child.* Speld Victoria, 1972.

Gurian, M. *The Minds of Boys.* Wiley, 2005.

Haddon, M. *The curious incident of the dog in the night-time.*
David Fickling Books, 2003.

Hall, N. A. *Rescue; A Handbook of Classroom Ideas to Motivate the*

Teaching of Remedial Reading. Educational Service Inc., 1969.

Hampshire, S. *Susan's Story; An Autobiographical Account of My Struggle with Words.* Sphere Books Ltd.

Happy, R.M. *Basketball Ball Handling.* Villa 8, 3 Isaac Place, Quakers Hill, NSW, 2763: Dribblers, 1995.

Hawke, M. *Activate Program.* Learning Connections, 2004.

Hawke, M. *Learning Connections, Teacher Education and Training.* Learning Connections, Latest edition 2005.

Hawke, M. *Nutrition and its Impact on Learning, Behaviour and Development.* Queensland, Australia: ANSUA, 1995.

Hawke, Maureen. *Learning Connections, Nutritional and Environmental Factors and How They Impact on Learning, Behaviour and Development.* Learning Connections Centre, Latest edition 2002.

Hawke, Maureen. *Learning Connections, The Movement Learning Connection.* Learning Connections Centre, Latest edition 2002.

Hayes, M. L. *The Tuned-In, Turned-On Book.* Academic Therapy Publications. 1974.

Hayward, I. and Neilson, M. *The Hyperkinetic Toddler.* England: Active-Hyperkinetic Children's Assn.

Herbert, C. *Noise and Movement.* Hyperactivity Association NSW, 1977.

Hewson, L. *When Half is Whole.* Dove Communications, 1982.

Hoermann, D. *A Developmental Music Programme (Kodaly based) Stage One.* A Dominie Publication, 1978.

Hoey, A. M. *Listening and Learning, The Development of Auditory Perception.* A Dominie Publication, 1977.

Holt, J. *How Children Learn.* Penguin Books, 1991.

Hoogstad, V. *Sounds and Silents*. Jacaranda Press, 1975.

Hoogstad, V. and L. *What's It All About?* The Jacaranda Press, 1978.

Hoogstad, V. and L. *You're Spellbound*. Cassell Australia, 1978.

Hooten, M. *The First Reading and Writing Book*.
Hill of Content, 1976.

Hornsby, B. *Overcoming Dyslexia; A straightforward guide for families and Teachers*. Australia: Methuen, 1984.

Hosking, G. *An Introduction to Paediatric Neurology*.
Faber and Faber Ltd., 1982.

Hyperactivity Association of South Australia. *What the Educator Should Know about Hyperactive Children*.

Irlen, Helen. *Reading By The Colors*, Penguin Putnum/Perigee Div.
USA, 1991.

Jansky, J. and de Hirsch, K. *Preventing Reading Failure–Prediction, Diagnosis, Intervention*. Harper and Row Publishers, 1972.

Jensen, E. *Different Brains, Different Learners*.
San Diego, California: The Brain Store, 2000.

Jensen, E. *Music with the Brain in Mind*.
San Diego, California: The Brain Store, 2000.

Jensen, E. *Teaching with the Brain in Mind 2nd Ed*. USA:
Association for Supervision and Curriculum Development, 2005.

Joudry, R. *Sound Therapy for the Walkman*. Steele and Steele, 1984.

Kaluger, G. and Kolson, C. J. *Reading and Learning Disabilities*.
Charles E. Merrill Publishing Co., 1969.

Kavanagh, J. F. and Mattingly, I. G. (editors). *Language by Ear and by Eye - The Relationships between Speech and Reading*.
M.I.T. Press, 1972.

Kephart, N. C. *The Slow Learner in the Classroom, 2nd Ed.* Charles Merrill Publishing Co., 1971.

Kirk, S. A. and Chalfant, J. C. *Academic and Developmental Learning Disabilities*, Love Publishing Company, Denver, 1984.

Kolson, C. J. and Kaluger, G. *Clinical Aspects of Remedial Reading.* Springfield, Illinois, USA: Charles C. Thomas, 1963.

Kottmeyer, W. *Teacher's Guide for Remedial Reading.* Webster Division, McGraw-Hill Book Co., 1959.

Kranowitz, C. S. *The Out of Sync Child Has Fun: Activities for Kids with Sensory Integration Dysfunction.* New York, NY: Perigee, 2003.

Krebs, C. T. *LEAP Brain Integration Course Manuals.* Melbourne, Australia: Melbourne Applied Physiology, 2004-2006.

Krebs, Dr. Charles. *A Revolutionary Way of Thinking.* Hill of Content, 1998.

Kronick, D. *A Word or Two about Learning Disabilities.* Academic Therapy Publications, 1973.

Kronick, D. *Social Development of Learning Disabled Persons.* Jossey-Bass Publishers, 1981.

Kronick, D. *They Too Can Succeed; A practical guide for Parents of Learning-Disabled Children.* Academic Therapy Publications, 1969.

Larkin, D. and Hoare, D. *Out of Step.* Nedlands, Western Australia: Department of Human Movement and Recreation Studies, University of Western Australia, 1991.

Laszlo, J. and Bairstow, P J. *Perceptual-Motor Behaviour, Developmental Assessment and Therapy.* Holt, Rinehart and Winston, 1985.

Le Winn, E.B. *Human Neurological Organisation.* Charles C. Thomas, 1969.

Leeds, J. *The Power of Sound*. Rochester, Vermont: Healing Arts Press, 2001.

Lefroy, Rob. *Improving Literacy through Motor Development*. Dunsborough Enterprises Pty. Ltd., 1990.

Lyon, Michael R. *Healing the Hyperactive Brain*. Focused Publishing, 2000.

MacDonald, T. H. *First Aid in Basic Mathematics; a handbook for parents and Teachers of children having difficulty with school mathematics*. Hale and Iremonger, 1983.

Mackarness, R. *Not all in the Mind*. London and Sydney: Pan Books, 1999.

McAllen, A. *The Extra Lesson*. Steiner Schools Fellowship Publications, 1985.

McDonald, Trudy and Paterson, Gail. *Learning Options, CHOICES FOR STRUGGLING STUDENTS*. BookSurge, LLC, 2006.

McElroy, C. W. *Speech and Language Development of the Pre-School Child*. Springfield, Illinois, USA: Charles C. Thomas, 1972.

Madaule, Paul. *When Hearing Comes Alive*. The Listening Centre, 1994.

Meillon, Ross and Reading, Chris. *Relatively Speaking*. Fontana, 1984.

Meiser, Frances. *The Brian Train*. CT, USA: Safe Goods, 1997.

Miles, T. R. *Understanding Dyslexia*. Hodder and Stoughton, 1974.

Millar, R. E. *Why is My Child Different?* Spectrum Publications, 1981.

Miller, Alice. *The Drama of the Gifted Child*. Basic Books, 1997.

Milne, D. *Teaching the brain to read*. SK Publishing, 2005.

Minchin, M. *Food for Thought. A Parent's Guide to Food Intolerance.*
Alma Publications, 1982.

Minde, K. *Parents' Guide to Hyperactivity.*
Quebec Assn. for Children with Learning Disabilities, 1988.

Myers, T. W. *Anatomy Trains.* Elsevier, 2001.

Nash-Wortham, M. and Hunt, J. *Take Time to 'Move in Time'.*
Fast-print Business Centre, 1986.

Noyes, J. and Macneill, N. *Your Child Can Win; Strategies, Activities and Games for Parents of Children with Learning Disabilities.*
Melbourne: Sun Books, 1983.

Nugent, C. *Three Dimensional Bead frame Mathematics.*
Victoria, Australia: Educo Services, 1985.

Nugent, C. *Write and Say, 1, 2 and 3.* Nelson, 1979.

O'Brien, C. *Movement and the Preschool Child.*
Dept of Education, Queensland, 1982.

O'Brien, C. and Ziviana, J. *Fine Motor Development and the Preschool Child.* Dept of Education, Queensland, 1984.

O'Hara, B. *Movement, the Brain and Learning Course notebook.*
Brighton, Victoria, Australia: 2006.

O'Hara, B. *Primitive and Postural Reflexes Course notebook.*
Brighton, Victoria, Australia: 2006.

Ornstein, R. *The Nature of Human Consciousness.*
San Francisco: W. H. Freeman & Co., 1978.

Ornstein, R. and Sobel, D. *The Healing Brain.* ISHK, 1999.

Owens, from talk by Dr. Wayne Wilson, Audiologist and Researcher, Queensland, Australia, SAMONAS Conference, Sydney, 2003.

Parker, A. and Cutler-Stuart, M. *Switch on Your Brain, A Guide to Better Reading, Concentration and Co-ordination*. Hale and Iremonger, 1986.

Pert, Candace B. *Molecules of Emotion*. Touchstone, 1997.

Pheloung, B. *Help Your Child to Learn, A practical guide for helping children with Learning Difficulties*. Bantam, Tortoiseshell Press, 1988.

Pheloung, B. and King, J. *Overcoming Learning Difficulties, How you can help a child who finds it hard to learn*. Doubleday, 1992.

Philpott, W. H. and Kalita, D. K. *Brain Allergies; The psychonutrient connection*. Keats Publishing, Inc., 1980.

Pollock, Joy and Waller, Elizabeth. *Day-to-Day Dyslexia in the Classroom, 2nd ed.* Routledge Falmer, 1997.

Pope, L. *Teaching Remedial Reading, revised 2nd Ed.* Book-Lab, Inc., 1975.

Porter L. *Educating Young Children with Special Needs* Allen & Unwin, Crows Nest Sydney, Australia, 2002.

Prosser, Dr Brenton. *ADHD who's failing who?Understanding the impact of ADHD on our young people, schools and society.* Finch Publishing Sydney, Australia, 2006.

Quin, V. and Macauslan, A. *Dyslexia; What parents ought to know.* Penguin Books, 1986.

Rawlings, B. *"just try darling"*. Quebec Association for Children with Learning Disabilities, 1980.

Richardson, P. *Fun Learning for Littlies.* Canberra Publishing and Printing Co., 1979.

Rie, H. E. and E. D. Editors. *Handbook of Minimal Brain Dysfunctions; a critical view.* John Wiley and Sons, 1980.

Rigby, J, *Children with Specific Learning Difficulties: ANSUA'S Approach*. ANSUA Learning Centre, 1994.

Rigby, J. and Hawke, M. *The ANSUA Developmental School Program*. Queensland: ANSUA Learning Centre.

Rotalo, S. K. *Right-brain Lesson Plans for a Left-brain World*. Charles C. Thomas, 1982.

Rothenberg, Mira. *Children with Emerald Eyes*. E. P Dutton, 1987.

Sasse, M. *If Only We'd Known...* Toddler Kindy Gymbaroo P.L., 1979.

Schneider, V. *Infant Massage; A Handbook for Loving Parents*. Bantam Books Inc, 2000.

Schragg, P. and Divoky, D. *The Myth of the Hyperactive Child*. Pelican Books, 1975.

Sheil, M. L. *The Importance of Being an Infant*. Toddler/Kindy Gym Pty. Ltd., 1984.

Sheridan, M. D. *Children's Developmental Progress; from birth to five years: the Stycar sequences, 5th imp*. NFER Publishing Company, 1977.

Sime, M. *A Child's Eye View; Piaget for young parents and Teachers*. London: Thames and Hudson, 1973.

Simpson, E. *Reversals, A Personal Account of Victory over Dyslexia*. London: Victor Gollancz Ltd., 1981.

Smith. S. L. *No Easy Answers: The L.D. Child*. U.S. Department of Health and Welfare, 1978.

Snowball, D. *Helping Your Child to Read. A guide for parents*. Thomas Nelson Australia, 1982.

Speech Pathology Department, The Parramatta Hospitals. *3 Pamphlets*. NSW, Australia: Westmead Centre.

Stehli, Annabel (ed). *Dancing in the Rain.*
The Georgiana Org. Inc., 1995.

Stehli, Annabel. *The Sound of a Miracle.*
Bantam, Dell and Doubleday, 1992.

Steinbach, I. *SAMONAS Sound Therapy: The Way to Health through Sound.* Kellinghausen, Germany: Techau Verlag, 1998.

Stott, D. H. *Roads to Literacy.* Holmes McDougall Ltd, 1964.

Stott, D. H. *The Parent as Teacher - A Guide for Parents of Children with Learning Difficulties.* University of London Press Ltd., 1974.

Tansley, A. E. *Identification Assessment Prescription.*
SPELD S.A. Inc., 1975.

Tansley, A. E. *Reading and Remedial Reading.*
London: Routledge and Kegan Paul, 1967.

Thomson, A. K. and Foreman, D. G. *Living English.* Jacaranda Press, 1966.

Tomatis, A. *The Conscious Ear.* New York: Station Hill Press, 1991.

Tortora, S. *The Dancing Dialogue.* Paul H. Brookes, 2006.

Vallett, R. E. *The Remediation of Learning Disabilities; a handbook of psychoeducational resource programs, 2nd ed.* Fearon Publishers, Inc.

Vayda, W. *Health for Life. Are you Allergic to the 20th Century?* Sphere Books, 1981.

Wagner, G., Hosier, M. and Blackman, M. *Listening Games; Building Listening Skills with Instructional Games.* A Grade Teacher Publication, 1960.

Walker, M. and Angelo, F. A. *Rebounding Aerobics.* National Institute of Reboundology and Health Inc., 1981.

Waller, E. *Dyslexia - The Problems of Handwriting. 1974, rev. ed. 1978*. London: The Helen Arkell Dyslexia Centre, 1978.

Walshe, R. D. *Every Child Can Write!, Learning and teaching written expression in the 1980s*. NSW, Australia: Primary English Teaching Association N.S.W., 1981.

Warnke, Ralph. *Central Processing and Automation Deficits.*

Watson, B. R. *Physical Education for Poorly Co-ordinated Children, the promotion of body awareness and the development of basic skills.* ACHPER Publications, 1984.

West, Thomas. *In The Mind's Eye.* New York, USA: Prometheus Books, 1977.

Westwood, Peter. *Spelling – Approaches to teaching and assessment.* Australia: Acer Press, 2005.

White, M., Lefroy, R. and Weston, D. *Treating Reading Disabilities.* Academic Therapy Publications, 1975.

Wiener, H. *Eyes okay I'm okay.* Academic Therapy Publications, 1977.

Wiig, E. H. and Semel, E. *Language Assessment and Intervention for the Learning Disabled, 2nd Ed.* Charles E. Merrill Publishing C9, 1984.

Wunderlich, R. C. *Kids, Brains and Learning- Update 1979, a collection of thoughts and writings prepared for ANSUA Australia.* July 1979.

Wunderlich, R. D. *Sugar and Your Health.* Good Health Publications, 1982.

Index

A

Academic testing: 109, 125
Addicts/addiction: 129, 93
Additives to food: 46, 50, 52, 53, 54, 55, 65, 172, 208, 209, 222, 228, anger from 55
ADHD: 64, 221, 230, 231
Almond, Mike: 242
Ambidextrous: 150
Amino acids: 63, 229
Anderson, Maxine: 7
Anger: 55, 131, 164, 231
ANSUA: 13, 93, 97, 282
Antibiotics: 232, 277, overuse 27, 47
Anxiety: 56, 63
Asperger's Syndrome: 62, 221, 233
Assessment (early): 206 - 207
Asymmetrical Tonic Neck Reflex: 75, 79, 80, 82, 83, 190
Asthma: 47, 56, 58 – 59, 62, 208, 224, 228, 236
and vegetarians 47
Auditory processing: 56, 57, 123, 124, 167 – 171, 198, 272
Autism: iv, 47, 62, 221, 223, 233, 280
Ayres, Dr. A. Jean: 13, 36, 39, 255, 280

B

Ball games: 181 - 188
Ballroom dancing: 196
Ball skills: 181 - 188
Barry, my husband: iii, 18, 39
Bat and ball: 186, 190
Batons: 189 - 190
Beach House: iv, 19 – 20, 21, 48, 116, 147, 148
Beal, Dr Susan: 34
Behaviour problems: 62, 102, 221, 226, 230 – 231, 280
Behavioural Optometrist: 10, 11, 34, 105, 109, 122, 131

Biochemical imbalances: 63, 231, 232
Bipolar disorder: 63, 230, 231
Blood analysis: 58, 59, 63, 225
Body Focus Therapy: 131
Body Righting Reflex: 77, 80
Bone conduction, sound therapy: 169
Bottrell, Perry: 10
Brain Gym: 107, 111, 123
Brain Integration: 12, 13, 14, 147, 180, 182, 273
Buddy system: 71, 139

C

Casein: 62, 233 - 235
Chapparo, Dr. Chris: 34, 89, 151, 156
Chemical intolerance: iv, 221, 228
Coeliac disease: 227, 229
Colic: 223, 236
Classical music, for listening: 130
Commonwealth Literacy Program: 97, 99 - 104
Computers: iii, xvii, 18, 101, 103, 201 - 202
Concentration: 44, 45, 48, 55, 75, 170, 224, 236
Convergence: 210, 275
Counselling adults: 127, 129, 131, 132
Cross-pattern/cross lateral flip flops: 58, 82, 96, 106, 110, 112, 123, 273
Cross-pattern/cross lateral crawling: xv, 15, 39, 58, 75, 81, 83, 85, 106, 110, 112, 123, 125, 129, 130, 162, 215, 217, 238, 273
Cross-pattern walking: 39, 86, 88, 110, 161, 162, 184, 273

D

Dancing (ballroom): 196
Delacato, Carl: vii, 13, 258
Dengate, Sue: 65, 208, 228, 258
Depression: 63, 199, 230, 231

V

Vestibular: 80, 124, 145, 147, 148, 150, 169, 272, 281, 282

Vision: 109, 169, 210 – 211, 271, 274, 279

Vision screening: 109, 124, 210 - 211

Visualising/verbalising: 111, 112, 256

Visually distracted: 161 – 162, 222, 274

Visual motor: 63, 153

Visual processing: 124, 167 – 168, 283

Vitamins: 58, 63, 209, 229 - 230

W

Water (drinking): 50, 56, 64, 125, 222

'White food': 53

Wunderlich, R.C.: vii, 269

Z

Zaremba, Barbara: 8

Zinc: 59, 224, 230 – 231, 235

Also available from Move to Learn

Books

Help Your Child to Learn

Not sure whether your underachiever has Learning Difficulties or not? Read this book first! *Help Your Child To Learn* will help you see where the immaturities are and outlines both the professional help required, and the order in which this help should be given.

THIRD EDITION
Over 22,000 copies sold!

Help Your Class to Learn

For classroom teachers and parents, *Help Your Class To Learn* outlines the reasons behind what we do and the importance of doing therapies in the right order. It also introduces specific movements and activities that will change strugglers into happy learners.

Overcoming Learning Difficulties

This book was written with the co-author Jill Taylor (King) a Paediatric Physiotherapist. It was written for all professionals involved in treating LD. Also excellent for keen parents anywhere. Many examples of simple activities to address each area of possible immaturity including trampoline sequences.

Other resources

Why and How to Get Started

A simple introduction on why and how to get started with the Move To Learn Program. Easy to read and informative, this booklet briefly sets out the thinking and research behind the program and convincingly introduces headmasters and decision makers to the benefits of this for children.

Move to Learn Brochure

A brief introduction to the Move To Learn Program. Many of the professionals involved in treating learning difficulties display these brochures in their clinics. Let us know the number of brochures you can use, so we can send them to you.

Move to Learn DVD/Video

This DVD/video shows parent and teacher interviews with the medical professionals needed to help those with LD. It also shows teachers doing a developmental sequence of nine movements retracing natural development, preparing their class for easier learning.

The program takes minimal preparation, – only DVD/Video and floorspace. *Move to Learn* only needs 15-20 minutes daily. The essential companion to *Help Your Class to Learn*.

Movement Posters

Large illustrated cards demonstrating the 9 sequenced movements featured in the 'Move to Learn' DVD/Video. For use in classroom or home, these are an excellent tool showing the exact requirements for each movement. Includes durable plastic envelope for storage.

Available online at www.movetolearn.net